**TAX**Cafe®

## Taxcafe.co.uk Property Guides

# How to Beat the Credit Crunch

## By Toby Hone

# Important Legal Notices:

Taxcafe®
PROPERTY GUIDE – "How to Beat the Credit Crunch"

**Published by:**
Taxcafe UK Limited
67 Milton Road
Kirkcaldy
KY1 1TL
United Kingdom
Tel: (01592) 560081

First Edition, July 2008

ISBN 1 904608 841

**Disclaimer**
Before reading or relying on the content of this guide, please read carefully the disclaimer on the last page which applies. If you have queries then please contact the publisher at team@taxcafe.co.uk.

# About The Author

My name is Toby Hone and I am a full-time landlord based in the UK. I graduated from the University of Cape Town with an honours degree in marketing and a major degree in economics and shortly thereafter began investing in property.

I have been investing for around 10 years now, initially in South Africa and subsequently in the UK and have built up a portfolio of 30 properties, valued at just shy of £3 million!

Unlike many property investors who stick to one thing, I have tried my hand successfully at a number of property investing disciplines, including:

- Buying new build properties at substantial discounts. These were not your typical city centre apartments which investment companies charge you an arm and a leg for. They were my personal homes which I managed to trade up to from a one-bedroom flat in the south east of London, when my wife and I first moved to the UK. My current residence is a five-bedroom ex-show home in Sherwood Forest, which I managed to buy at a 'real' discount of 25%!

- Refurbishing repossessions. This has involved buying properties through estate agents and auctions which are in such a state of disrepair that most potential buyers don't even get through the front door. This has been my 'bread and butter' in recent years and I've found it relatively easy to build my portfolio by investing in this type of property.

- Buying freehold properties which are already separated into a number of self-contained units, splitting each unit onto its own leasehold title and remortgaging each unit.

- Developing – not your builder from scratch type developments but rather unique schemes where the shell of a building is kept but the interior is re-designed to achieve multiple units, with each put onto a separate leasehold and remortgaged.

- Letting many properties to many tenants!

This property guide has been compiled using input from a number of professional landlords, solicitors and mortgage brokers, each specialising in different areas and with unique insights into the key areas that impact a landlord.

I look forward to receiving your comments and feedback and I hope the guide will give you some practical insights into the many different ways of improving the cash position of your property portfolio. The various ideas should help save you thousands of pounds and ultimately help you survive and beat the credit crunch.

**If one thing is certain it is that the coming months will be uncertain!** Because of this landlords need to ensure they are managing their portfolios efficiently. The risk is that many investors could find themselves in serious financial difficulty if property prices keep falling and interest rates keep rising.

The drought of good mortgage deals and increasingly strict lending criteria will have a severe impact on many landlords mortgage payments over the next 12–18 months. If measures are not taken now to improve portfolio cash positions, many landlords risk losing everything!

At the time of writing this guide the UK buy-to-let market is undergoing tremendous upheaval. Lenders are trying to recoup huge losses which resulted from making disastrous investments linked to sub-prime mortgages in the US. Lenders have been forced to save their cash to repair their balance sheets.

Banks are extremely nervous about lending and are continually increasing their mortgage rates and tightening their credit criteria which has resulted in the number of mortgage approvals almost halving in the last year.

This guide will highlight the key areas that landlords need to focus on to ensure their survival in the coming months. It also identifies the major risks faced by landlords and provides practical and useful tips on how to deal with these threats and improve the cash position of your property portfolio.

Please feel free to send me your feedback and suggestions!


**Enjoy the Book!**

**Toby Hone**

# Dedication

This book is dedicated to my wife.

Sone, thank you for all your support, love and patience and for helping me keep my Faith!

I could not have done it without you!

# Contents

# Introduction

# **My Story**

**I**t has always amazed me how the media has for many years endorsed the view that it is relatively easy to make money by investing in property...

... but they never show you how to **manage a portfolio**.

After all, it is one thing to buy properties but quite another to actively manage a portfolio with a view to maximizing rental yields or re-structure your portfolio to bolster either your equity, rental income, or both!

Chats at social gatherings, including the local pub, usually include talk of how someone has built up a property portfolio worth millions, or how someone else has made thousands of pounds buying and selling a property in very little time and with very little effort.

I have to admit that even I was lured into paying a ridiculous amount of money to attend one of those seminars where, for virtually two whole days, I was given a vaguely disguised sales pitch on how to buy over-priced apartments.

I remember how a property tycoon, boasting about his rise to riches, and driving his new Bentley (or was it a Rolls Royce?), told everyone they can make millions just like him – all they have to do is buy property!

I say this because I can relate to anyone who has fallen for the sales pitch and bought this type of property, lured by the prospect of not having to put down any deposit.

However, I learnt some important lessons through my own research and experience of the UK housing and mortgage markets, which allowed me to quickly build up a substantial property portfolio using my own techniques.

Unlike many landlords who hold onto their day jobs, early on I took the plunge and became a full-time property investor. I had a baby on the way, lived in a tiny one-bed flat in the south east of London and had very little money to play with.

As a result, I was forced to spend a lot of time looking for the right kind of property to buy. I was worried that if I screwed up my first purchase I would have to go back to my day job. Now that certainly motivated me!

As things turned out, I ended up buying a property in the East Midlands (I could barely afford the deposit on properties in London) and made enough money from this deal to set myself up in my property career.

Since then I have largely followed the same formula: purchasing properties in a state of disrepair, usually at auction or through re-possession, refurbishing them, renting them out, and remortgaging.

This strategy has given me the best of both worlds – I have been able to build up a property portfolio with substantial equity, while at the same time earning a good rental income.

Along the way I have had to learn how to manage my portfolio more efficiently and this is where many of the tips included in this guide come from.

However, there is a saying that one of my good friends, John Roussot, an entrepreneur and author often quotes: "If you are not growing, you are dying!" This has never been more true than in today's current financial and economic climate.

I first realized that trouble was on the horizon when mortgage brokers started murmuring about various staple lenders pulling their products.

I had four properties lined up to buy and was ready to exchange and complete (I have found that simultaneous exchange and completion works well when buying properties requiring refurbishment) when my broker called to tell me that, not only had rates suddenly gone up, but my mortgage offers had been withdrawn!

That was quite a reality check. Not only did I lose all my fees associated with the initial purchase proceedings, I was now not going to make any money from these deals. So I decided to shift my focus. If I could no longer make money from refurbishing properties, I was going to have to look at other techniques.

This proved a challenge with all the changes taking place in the mortgage market. However, I eventually found my next few projects, the first of which was the conversion of a detached housing office in Lincoln into three separate two-bedroom flats. This was bigger than the type of refurbishment I was used to but the numbers made sense so I decided to go for it. I will provide a more detailed overview of these projects later in the book.

I also had to change the way I financed projects, an area that is almost always ignored by TV pundits and many authors.

The important point to note, however, is that I took a close look at my existing situation and changed my investment strategy to work in the current climate.

# CHAPTER 1

# Understanding Your Position

The two most important facets of any property portfolio are:

- The amount of equity you hold, and

- The amount of rental profit or loss you make

Taken together these show the overall health of your portfolio. If you're making substantial rental profits and have substantial equity, your portfolio is very healthy. However, if you're making heavy rental losses and have little or no equity, your portfolio is extremely unhealthy.

Most landlords are sitting in one of the four quadrants of the Landlord Health Check diagram (Figure 1). Now in order to decide your best strategy going forward, it's essential to identify which quadrant you're sitting in.

For instance, if you have Low Equity and Rental Losses, your goal will perhaps be to improve your existing rental loss position by aggressively targeting reductions in operating costs, maximizing rental yields, self management of your portfolio and, where possible, selling properties that offer scope to release equity.

*Figure 1. Landlord Health Check Diagram*

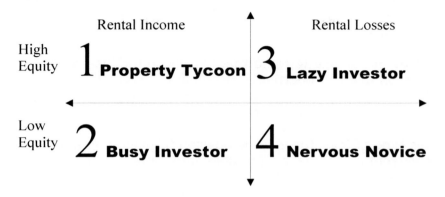

## The Four Quadrants

The four quadrants shown in the Landlord Health Check Diagram can be summarized as follows:

**1 – Property Tycoon** – These investors have very little debt relative to the value of their properties. They also have very strong rental income which allows them to continue investing or to shore up cash reserves for hard times. This is the position where most property investors would like to end up.

A decline in property values, like we're currently experiencing, will not worry many of these landlords, in fact many of them see it as a golden opportunity to sweep up bargains when the market starts to recover. This group stand to make a lot of money when this happens.

Property Tycoons are also benefiting from strong income growth, as more and more people look to rent rather than buy, which pushes up rental yields. This type of landlord will be looking forward to the coming years.

**2 – Busy Investor** - This group of landlords is more highly geared but still has significant rental income which gives them some comfort in the current market conditions.

This would include many student landlords and House in Multiple Occupation (HMO) landlords. Because they are relatively highly geared they are susceptible to prolonged decreases in house prices.

If they are unable to remortgage because the loan to value ratio on their properties is too high, they will have to absorb higher mortgage costs which will eat up their rental income and could push them into the 4th Quadrant.

This type of investor may be advised to plough as much of their rental income as possible into either a drawdown mortgage facility, or to shore up cash reserves in case they are forced to switch to their lender's Standard Variable Rate (SVR).

**3 – Lazy Investor** – This investor is perhaps unfairly called lazy, however I will explain the reason for this. If you have substantial equity but are making rental losses, you should be putting more effort into maximizing your returns. Otherwise you would possibly be better off selling the portfolio and investing the money in a high interest savings account.

If you continue making rental losses, while in the current market the value of your properties falls, you will be losing money on two fronts: both capital and income.

This group of landlords typically use letting agents to manage their portfolios and because of this lose out on potential rental profits because of the high management charges. They're possibly also not achieving the maximum possible rent.

Frankly, this type of landlord should be focusing on improving rental yields, reducing operating costs and selling those properties that contribute most to the rental losses (assuming they are happy to pay capital gains tax). They should then use the proceeds from these sales to build up cash reserves or use the money to invest in properties that offer more scope to earn rental profits.

**4 – Nervous Novice** – This is by far the worst position to be in. These landlords, of which there are many, will be seriously worried about their financial future. With decreasing house prices, the likelihood of obtaining competitive remortgages is very small, which means they will have to stick with their lender's standard variable rate, which will result in much higher mortgage costs.

The fact they're making rental losses means this group of landlords will also be heavily subsidizing their property portfolios out of other income. Unless they have access to large amounts of cash, or have extremely high earnings, the medium-term outlook is bleak and many will go bust if they don't act now!

These landlords include those who bought off-plan discounted properties and city centre flats which offer little scope for improving rental yields in the short term. With property prices decreasing there's only a very slim chance they will make any money by selling.

This group of investors also includes those who were lured into buying property by the plethora of property programmes that swept onto our television screens between 2005–2007. These shows boasted how anyone and their dog could make money in property but most only paid lip service to the fact that money was being made purely because the market was rising so strongly and could reverse in a short space of time.

People in the position of the Nervous Novice will need to apply the principles in this book the most. They will have to be creative in finding ways to increase rental yields by finding the best types of tenants and making their properties the most desirable to live in.

They will have to focus on self managing their portfolios in every respect to minimize costs and ensure deposits are protected and big enough so no losses result from damages or unpaid rent.

This group of investors will also have to slash their personal spending and find ways to shore up cash reserves. And they will have to do this fast!

## Planning Your Property Strategy

Once you have identified what type of landlord you are and your portfolio's current health you will be in a much better position to establish your strategy going forward. There are also other considerations that will impact your strategy including:

- Your medium and long-term goals (both personal and investment)
- Your existing earnings
- Your access to financial resources
- Your lifestyle

It's easy to see that a millionaire Property Tycoon may have different investment goals to a Lazy Investor. Indeed their lifestyles will probably also be different. These considerations may appear vague, however let me run two scenarios by you:

**Scenario 1**: Dave is 57 and has paid off his house which is worth £400,000. He has built up a property portfolio worth £2 million over a three year period on which he has mortgages of £1.5 million. He is currently breaking even on the rental side (which includes letting agent fees) and has five years to go before he retires.

**Scenario 2**: John is 35 and has an 85% mortgage on his house which is worth £400,000. He has built up a property portfolio worth £2 million over a three year period on which he has mortgages of £1.5 million. Like Dave he is also currently breaking even on the rental side (including letting agent fees).

Now, other than the difference in their ages and the size of the mortgage on their homes, these two landlords appear to be in the same position.

However, looking at Dave, he only has three years to go until he retires. If he adopts the strategy of riding out the credit crunch and the resulting fall in house prices, he stands to lose substantial sums of money.

Assuming an average 30% reduction in house prices over a 3 year period (we'll return to this assumption later!), he will lose £120,000 on his primary residence and £600,000 on his buy-to-let portfolio – a total loss of £720,000!

This is a disaster for him because he may have originally planned to sell the buy-to-let properties at a healthy profit to boost his retirement income. Because he has a shorter time horizon he may not be able to hang on long enough for prices to recover.

When he retires and his earnings drop he may also struggle to remortgage his properties at competitive interest rates. He could then end up with significant rental losses but insufficient earnings to cover them now that he has retired. The end result is he may have to continue working or even sell his home to make ends meet.

John, on the other hand, does not have to worry about imminent retirement. He might take the view that his properties will eventually rise again in value and go on to make healthy capital gains.

He could quite feasibly switch his primary residential mortgage onto a long-term fixed-rate deal and maximize his rental returns by managing the portfolio himself and increasing the rental income in a disciplined fashion. This way he can minimize the adverse effect of higher buy-to-let interest rates.

Clearly Dave and John are in the same position when it comes to the overall health of the portfolio. However, they have different time horizons and future earnings capability. John has time on his side and can potentially ride out any property price crash and still achieve his long-term goal of financial independence.

It's important to stress that, in order to develop your own strategy going forward, you need to look seriously at the health of your existing property portfolio and take account of your medium and long-term goals, your earnings capability, your other financial resources and your overall lifestyle.

Throughout this book many practical tips will be given to help you improve the health of your portfolio. However, it's just as important to balance these tips against your personal circumstances.

To put it bluntly, if you are living beyond your means, accumulating debt, and your portfolio is 'unhealthy' you will need to make serious adjustments, not only to your lifestyle, but to the way you manage your portfolio.

Many people will feel like the Nervous Novice. They will be losing money each month on the rental side and will have little or no equity in their portfolios.

If you find yourself in this position, it is still possible to get through the credit crunch, however you will need to make some drastic changes and improvements.

*I wish you all the best and I am confident that if you apply many of the ideas mentioned in this book you will greatly improve your chances of beating the credit crunch!*

# CHAPTER 2

# Key Target Areas

There are a few key areas property investors need to target to improve the health of their property portfolios:

- Mortgages
- Rent
- Deposits
- Operating costs

Before taking a look at each of these factors I'd like to briefly discuss the outlook for the UK property market.

## Property Market Outlook

In order to understand the current situation with regards to the property market and the mortgage market it is necessary to consider the factors that led up to the credit crunch, what the expected outcome will be, and also to understand the current UK housing market.

It is also necessary to compare the US housing market with the UK housing market and understand the differences and similarities. Below is a table comparing key statistics for the UK and the US housing markets.

## Table 1 – Comparison between UK & US Housing Markets

| Key Statistics | UK | USA |
|---|---|---|
| Population | 61 million | 301 million |
| Average salary | £25,000 | $50,000 |
| Number of houses | 24.5 million (total) 17 million (owner occupied) | 106 million (total) 55 million (owner occupied) |
| People per house | 2.5 | 2.8 |
| Houses rented | 7.8 million | 34 million |
| % of total houses rented | 32% | 32% |
| Average property price | £185,000 | $200,000 |
| Price / Earnings Ratio | 7 | 4 |
| Est. Number of Repossessions 2008 | 80,000 | 1.9 million |
| Number of Repossessions 2008 as % of population | 0.13% | 0.65% |
| Number of Repossessions as % of house total | 0.33% | 1.84% |
| Value of Repossessions | £14.8 billion | $389.4 billion |
| Total value of Housing market | £4.5 trillion | $21.2 trillion |
| Unemployment | 1.6 million | 8.5 million |
| Unemployment % | 5% | 5.50% |
| Number of mortgage holders | 12 million | 39 million |
| Houses not mortgaged | 12.5 million | 16.5 million |
| Owner Occupied Units | 17.2 million | 55.2 million |
| % of total housing | 70% | 52.09% |
| Avg. Monthly Mortgage payment on mortgaged houses | £572 | $1,088 |
| Median Gross Rent | £1,004 | $777 |
| Households with home equity lines of credit | | 7,2 million |
| New Home Sales 2008 | 40,680 | 512,000 |
| Household debt as % to income | 173% | 130% |
| Residential mortgages outstanding | £1.2 trillion | $3 trillion |
| Average Household mortgage | £100,451 | $77,592 |
| Sub-prime mortgages to increase as ARM ends in 2008 | | 1.8 million |
| Total Sub-prime mortgages | - | 3 million |
| Average value of sub-prime mortgage | - | $180,000 |
| Total value of sub-prime mortgage | - | $540 billion |
| Average LTV | 44% | - |
| Mortgages at 80% or above LTV | 500,000 | - |
| % of total housing at 80% LTV | 2.04% | - |
| % of total mortgages at 80% LTV | 4.17% | - |

*Data for Table 1 is extracted from various sources:*

- *Council of Mortgage Lenders*
- *US Housing Bureau*
- *National Association of Home Builders*
- *UK Statistics Authority*

As can be seen, the USA has just under five times the population of the UK and the average salary is almost identical, when converted into the same currency.

The number of people per property (2.84 and 2.48 respectively) is also similar and the percentage of houses rented is identical (32% in both the UK and US).

One of the most startling differences is the average house price, with UK prices almost double those in the US.

The price to earnings ratio, which represents broad affordability, shows that in the UK house prices are 7 times the average annual salary, while in the US they are 4 times the average annual salary.

This is one of the most serious issues facing the UK housing market and has arisen due to lenders being able to source cheap finance and offer mortgages with high loan to value ratios (LTVs) and at large multiples to income.

Looking at the effect of the credit crunch, the total number of repossessions in the US is likely to be 1.9 million in 2008. It's getting to the point where almost one out of every 100 Americans is going to have their house repossessed.

The rate of repossessions is five times higher in the US than in Britain. This may be a sign of the relative resilience of the UK housing market. Or it may be because we haven't seen the worst of the credit crunch yet.

Perhaps the most worrying figure from the USA's perspective is that 1.8 million more sub-prime borrowers are due to come off their adjustable rate mortgages (ARMs) in 2008!

As an expected new wave of repossessions hits the USA, lenders with exposure to these mortgages will begin a new round of write-offs. The effect will be to even further depress the US housing market which seems to be caught in a downward spiral.

There are 3 million houses owned by sub-prime borrowers with a total value of $540 billion. However, this is just 3% of the total number of houses in the US, so it's startling how much impact the sub-prime mortgage meltdown has had on the global economy.

It's important to bear in mind what's going on in the US when looking at the UK housing market. With at least 500,000 mortgages in the UK sitting at 80% loan to value or worse, and an estimated 1.2 million mortgages coming to the end of their fixed rate deals in 2008, there is a serious risk that the number of repossessions will grow like it has in the US.

Combining this with the fact that UK houses are 7 times the average person's income, mortgages have dried up, mortgage rates have been increased and are expected to increase further if inflation keeps rising, and you have a deadly cocktail that poses a serious threat to UK landlords and property investors.


## Household Debt

Another potentially lethal addition to this credit crunch cocktail is the fact that household debt as a percentage of income is at the highest level it has ever been – 173%. In the US it's 130%.

*Figure 2. Real House Prices 1975-2008*

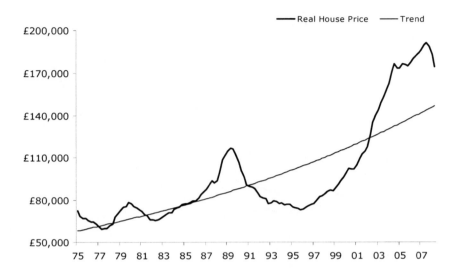

Source: Nationwide Building Society

High household debt increases the probability of a major house price correction. As rising prices and potential interest rate rises bite into the average person's disposable income, there is less money to service household debt, potentially resulting in more house repossessions.

## Real House Prices

Figure 2 illustrates real house price growth in the UK from 1975 up to 2008.

Although house prices have historically gone up, and are expected to continue this trend in the long term, the correction over the next three to ten years could be significant.

*Figure 3. Real House Prices 2007-2023?*

The correction which took place in the early 1990s lasted for 12 years! The economic and financial backdrop was different then – interest rates, for one, were around 15%.

However, two factors which indicate there is further trouble brewing for the UK housing market are **unemployment** and the **average house price to earnings ratio**.

Unemployment was initially 6.8% in 1990. However, this had increased to 10% within four years as the full effect of the housing crash rippled through the economy.

Looking at 2008, already unemployment is increasing rapidly as builders stop new projects, building suppliers have less demand for materials, contractors associated with the building trade lose work, estate agents shut up shop, banking firms lay off staff and streamline operations, and removal firms close down... the list of affected companies goes on and on.

Also, the fact that house prices were 4.5 times income in the 1990s, compared with an average of 7 times today, means that any pro-longed increase in interest rates could severely affect the UK housing market even more.

Looking at Figure 2, when the last correction took place in 1990, house prices dropped roughly 35% over a period of five years. It took another seven years thereafter for prices to reach the same levels as 1990.

Figure 3 is purely hypothetical. It shows what would happen if the 1990s property crash was transported to the present day. What the graph shows is that IF the current downturn in the property market turns out to be as severe as it was in the 1990s, you won't see property values recover to their recent highs until around 2020!

Indications are that with personal debt at record levels, if interest rates stay high for a prolonged period or even increase, then many people with a mortgage, including landlords, won't be in a position to meet their monthly payments which will probably lead to mass repossessions and further house price drops.


## In Summary

This is obviously a simplistic overview and the economic factors and circumstances are different now than in the 1990s.

However, there's no doubt that the current financial crisis is very severe.

Banks and their investors will carry the hangover from the credit binge with them for many years and this will no doubt affect their ability and willingness to lend.

The bottom line is that UK house prices could be in line for a major correction and the UK landlord needs to adopt a strategy to mitigate the potential damage.

## Credit Card Debt

Another area of concern is the level of UK credit card debt. There are more credit cards in the UK than people – 72 million!

People are increasingly using credit cards to subsidise increases in living costs and this is likely to lead to a new wave of credit problems as people struggle to meet their monthly repayments.

If this happens en masse the ensuing chaos will be severe. Lenders will have to write off a whole new wave of debt and this could further tighten up any funds available for the mortgage market.

There are many similarities between the US and UK, however, the problem is bigger in the UK because the percentage of household debt to income is far greater.

Some argue that the UK has sound economic fundamentals such as low unemployment (5%). However, the US has only slightly higher unemployment (5.5%).

Unemployment is expected to increase in the UK as companies in sectors hard hit by the credit crunch begin to lay off staff and restructure. As already mentioned, unemployment reached 10% by 1994 from levels of 6.8% in 1990.

The people that become unemployed will no doubt have difficulty in meeting their mortgage repayments and with UK growth slowing new jobs will not be created fast enough to absorb the increasing numbers of unemployed.

The result could be a huge increase in the number of repossessions.

The effect on banks that have to lay off staff to reduce their costs to compensate for write-offs of US sub prime debt will also impact unemployment and City bonuses that were the primary driver of London house price growth will dry up.

This will eventually feed through, as it historically has, to the rest of the UK property market.

## Sub-Prime Debts

Some banks have estimated the total sub-prime losses will top $1 trillion!

The UK currently has only 500,000 mortgages with LTVs of 80% or more. However, this assumes that valuations are accurate, which many buy-to-let investors will know is not the case.

The proliferation of below market value (BMV) deals and gifted deposits from builders, which rely on elements of over-valuation to source finance with minimum deposit, means that many new-build city centre apartments which were over-valued at the time of being purchased will need to be classified as above 80% LTV.

BMV deals have involved buying property from distressed sellers prepared to sell their homes at a discount and rent them back. Investors who do these deals have relied on high valuations to remortgage properties and extract extra cash from lenders.

Banks realized that they were exposing themselves to a new threat by lending to landlords who were ultimately renting their properties to risky tenants who had been forced to sell their homes because they were in financial difficulty.

## Buy-to-Let Sector

Looking specifically at the UK buy-to-let (BTL) sector, the figures are vague as not all lenders that offer BTL mortgages submit their data to the Council of Mortgage Lenders (CML).

According to the CML there were 1.1 million BTL mortgages as of April 2008. According to *The Guardian* there are over one million landlords in the UK and one of the largest BTL lenders, Mortgage Express, says that the average landlord has between 1 and 5 properties.

It is also worth noting that research carried out by Mintel suggests that 3% of all UK homeowners in the UK are considering purchasing a rental property by 2010, and if this happens the number of expected landlords will be two million.

The UK population is currently estimated to be just over 60 million and is expected to grow to 65 million by 2016. This means that there is an average of 2.4 people per home.

It is also worth noting that there are currently 22 million single person households and this number is expected to grow to 26 million by 2016 and contribute the most to the increase in housing required.

## Upside

There is, however, a longer term upside to the current financial crisis. A number of home builders, including the UK's largest, Persimmon Homes, announced in May 2008 that they would be freezing all plans for future projects of new build homes while the mortgage famine remains.

The reason for this is that they are unable to find buyers, as people now have to find much higher deposits and cannot afford bigger mortgage payments. You may ask how this is good news.

New home starts registered with the NHBC are almost 1/3 lower than last year. Bearing in mind that the Government has set itself a target of building 2 million new homes by 2016 (roughly 250,000 per year) the current building slowdown means that these targets will not be met.

These Government targets were formulated by taking into consideration factors that influence housing demand, such as demographic changes including population growth, longer life expectancy, the growth of single parent families, higher divorce rates and immigration.

Although inflation is bad for the economy it may force wages up and make house prices more affordable.

Combining a levelling off in the supply of houses with demographic changes, along with higher than average wage increases, there could be a return to house price growth sooner than expected.

This does however rely entirely on the availability and supply of finance at reasonable interest rates. When liquidity eventually returns to the mortgage market, there could be a tremendous amount of pent up demand.

In the meantime falling house prices will convert into higher demand for rental properties and this represents an opportunity to landlords in the short to medium term.

## House Price Growth

The only way that house price growth will return is if confidence returns to the housing sector and this will only happen when the economy improves, inflation stabilizes, and finance becomes more readily available again.

However, banks are likely to remain stricter in their lending practices, and the cost of borrowing may remain higher than it has been for many years. There are encouraging signs though as some banks are already starting to reduce interest rates on some mortgage products to boost their lending as the demand for mortgages has severely tapered off in the last 12 months.

The biggest unknown is whether banks will continue this trend in light of inflation and the outlook for interest rates.

# CHAPTER 3

# Mortgages

## Where are Mortgages Heading?

The biggest single cost for most landlords is mortgage interest. No one can accurately predict where interest rates will be in a year's time, however, it's important to recognize that there is a risk that mortgage rates will be even higher in a year's time.

I'm not saying interest rates ARE going to rise... but there is always that danger and landlords should always prepare for the worst.

Many property investors will be busy with new purchases or remortgaging existing properties and with the dwindling number of products available it is critical to choose the correct course going forward.

One of the biggest choices you have to make is between a fixed and variable rate mortgage. It is also important to know what's the best timeframe for either fixing or taking a variable rate mortgage.

I must stress that it is also vitally important to discuss your borrowing requirements with a mortgage professional.

Many investors are unsure as to where mortgage rates are heading. Banks on the other hand have already made up their minds. SWAP rates have edged up for the past eight months and this is illustrated by the fact that in June 2007 it was relatively easy to get an 85% buy to let mortgage at an interest rate of 5.44% fixed for two years.

The current situation is that the best rates available now are around 6.85% with LTVs of 75% and the majority of lenders have withdrawn products, and some have even quit the buy-to-let sector altogether.

## Future Projections

Looking ahead to a year from now (when many investors who purchased using two-year fixed-rate deals will be looking to remortgage) the outlook does not look promising. The Bank of England has already indicated, as has the Federal Reserve, that inflation is starting to present a real threat and interest rate increases have not been ruled out.

Landlords will have to make an educated guess as to what they believe is going to happen to mortgage rates but it's important to stress that it's almost impossible to predict what will happen.

Perhaps more important is to plan your affairs so your property portfolio can withstand an interest rate shock. This could involve taking out a fixed-rate mortgage now or building up a cash reserve if you have existing variable rate mortgages.

## Plan for the Worst

My personal belief is that it is always best to plan for the worst, rather than planning for the best. At least by covering yourself against the worst outcome you know what the maximum impact will be on your cash flow and you can take the relevant precautions to overcome this.

*Figure 4. Impact of Interest Rate Changes*

Although it's impossible to accurately predict what will happen to interest rates, it's worth having a look at the impact that incremental increases in rates will have on your mortgage payments.

## Impact of Interest Rate Changes on Your Portfolio

Figure 4 illustrates the effect that incremental increases in interest rates will have on a property valued at £120,000 with an 85% mortgage of £102,000.

With rental coverage of 110% the property is earning rental income of £537 per month and the monthly mortgage payment is £488.75, based on an interest rate of 5.75%.

If we consider that at the time of writing this guide, lenders have raised their mortgage rates to an average of 7%, the impact would be a rental loss of £58 per month. If mortgage interest rates rise by another 1% to 8% the net monthly loss for this property would be £143!

If you then apply this to a property portfolio of 10 properties, the monthly loss would be £1,430, or £17,160 per year! This example shows how relatively modest increases in interest rates could eat up your rental income and leave you significantly out of pocket.

The situation is made worse when you consider the added effect of falling house prices on loan to value ratios (LTVs). If house prices fall substantially over a long period, there will be serious risks for many landlords who have relatively high loan to value ratios. When their fixed term mortgages expire, they may have no option but to switch to high standard variable rates (SVRs).

This should make you realize just how important it is to ensure you are managing your portfolio efficiently. Those landlords who fail to do this will risk financial ruin!

## The UK's Own Home Grown Credit Crunch

Many landlords will consider any fall in house prices to be a temporary problem which can be overcome by merely holding on to a property until it increases in value again. After all, landlords typically buy property for long-term capital gains and in recent years growth has always lived up to expectations.

However, the last housing downturn in the 1990s resulted in a severe fall in property prices (over 30% in just a few short years) and it took around 8 years for prices to recover to their previous levels.

The important thing to realise from a landlord's perspective is that, as house prices fall, so the loan to value (LTV) rises. If a landlord has an LTV of 85% and house prices then fall 10%, he will be left with an LTV of roughly 95%.

If you then consider that lenders have been, and are expected to continue, tightening their lending criteria, the many landlords who currently have loan to value's of 80% or more, will not be able to remortgage in a year's time!

In fact, if property prices fall heavily over the next two years then even landlords with healthy portfolios may struggle to remortgage and obtain a good fixed-rate deal. For example, if you have 10 properties worth £1 million with total mortgages of £600,000, if prices fall 25% over the next two years your portfolio will be worth just £750,000. Your loan to value ratio will jump from a relatively healthy 60% to 80%. As a result you may not qualify for many lenders remortgage deals which require LTVs of 75% or less.

This is a serious threat – landlords unable to remortgage due to not having enough equity in their portfolios will be forced to stay with their existing lenders and switch to sometimes extortionate standard variable rates (SVRs).

This will mean increases in mortgage payments of up to 50%! It is very unlikely that landlords will be able to increase their rents by anything close to this amount and will have to rely on their other financial resources. Those who cannot cover their rental  losses out of other income will eventually have their properties repossessed.

To further complicate matters, lenders are quite within their rights, as is spelled out in their terms and conditions, to ask the borrower for an additional deposit to bring the mortgage back in line with their required LTV.

Hence, if upon remortgaging a lender takes a view that your property has dropped in value by 10%, and your original LTV was 85%, they are quite within their rights to request you pay them 10% of the property's current value (£10,000 on a property worth £120,000) to bring the LTV back to its required level!

If this were to happen, I doubt very many landlords would be in a position to be able to pay out such large sums to lenders and would be inclined to either try and sell their properties, or let them be repossessed.

It is worth noting, however, that lenders will no doubt have a significant number of properties falling into this type of 'marginal equity' situation and probably realise that by trying to force landlords to bring LTVs back into line, they may cause their very own asset book collapse, as large numbers of properties would have to be sold in a hurry and many loans would not be repaid in full.

## Getting the Full Picture

I'm often surprised how many landlords don't know what mortgage products are available or the differences between the various types of mortgage.

You have to get hold of this information if you want to beat the credit crunch. Ineffective mortgage planning could leave you extremely vulnerable to certain economic and financial events in the months ahead.

For example:

- If interest rates rise to double digits, will you be able to keep paying the bank?

- If house prices have dropped by 20% when it's time for you to remortgage, but lenders are only offering 75% LTV mortgages, what will you do?

- How will you cope with being forced onto the lender's standard variable rate (SVR) mortgage?

The number of mortgage products available in the UK has dropped by 75% over the last year! This is a dramatic change and it's likely additional products will be withdrawn in the months ahead.

# Understanding Mortgages

The following is an overview of the various types of mortgage available. These mortgages can typically be used for your home as well as buy-to-let properties. Experienced landlords may wish to skip this section.

## Variable Rate Mortgages

Your mortgage payments will depend upon your lender's standard variable rate (SVR) and this has historically been closely linked to the Bank of England base rate. However, thanks to the credit crunch and the shortage of money, some lenders have actually *increased* their SVRs, even when the Bank of England was *lowering* interest rates.

Banks are not obliged to pass on Bank of England rate cuts unless you have what's known as a tracker mortgage – a mortgage whose interest rate tracks the Bank of England base rate.

Many lenders SVRs are now on average 2% higher than the Bank of England base rate. However, SVRs do vary significantly between different lending institutions so it is worth looking around to find the most competitive deal.

*Advantages of Variable Mortgages:*

- These are the most common type of mortgage and therefore the most competitive and can often work out the cheapest.

*Disadvantages of Variable Mortgages:*

- There an element of uncertainty. With the rate of inflation accelerating it is possible interest rates will be increased in the months ahead. This will mean higher interest payments for all those with variable rate mortgages. If the Bank of England raises interest rates significantly many buy-to-let investors will be unable to cover the shortfall between their rental income and mortgage interest.

## Fixed Rate Mortgages

This type of mortgage offers the most protection against interest rate increases. If certainty is what you want then go for a fixed-rate mortgage. They usually last for periods of two to five years.

*Advantages of Fixed Rate Mortgages:*

- Ideal if you want the certainty of a fixed monthly payment.

- Most useful when interest rate increases are expected, especially if a big increase could mean that you are unable to meet your mortgage payments and therefore could lose your property.

- Gives you control over your costs – you know exactly what your mortgage payments will be over the fixed term of the loan. If you then factor in regular increases in rental income (even a small amount each year) you may be able to gradually turn rental losses into rental profits.

*Disadvantages of Fixed Rate Mortgages:*

- You will not benefit from any cuts in interest rates.

- Banks are also worried that the Bank of England will increase interest rates in the near future so they're charging a premium to those customers who want the certainty of a fixed rate. In other words, interest rates on fixed-rate mortgages are usually higher than for variable rate mortgages. Arrangement fees are also higher.

- Fixed-rate mortgages usually come with heavy redemption penalties or charges should you wish to change or pay off your mortgage before the end of the fixed term. These can range from hundreds of pounds up to many thousands of pounds. This is a critical factor to consider when deciding your mortgage strategy. Big redemption penalties could prevent you from selling a property that you would otherwise want to offload.

Even the best economists in the country have different views on interest rates. For this reason it's probably sensible for most landlords to commit to a fixed rate for the certainty this provides. The rate may be quite high but at least it's not in double digits! With this in mind you can then focus on improving your portfolio's health through operating cost reductions and improving rental yields.

**Capped Mortgages**

These are a combination of fixed and variable rate mortgages.

They're similar to fixed rate mortgages in that, if the base rate rises, your mortgage rate won't go above a certain level. However, like a variable rate mortgage, if the base rate falls you can still benefit from a reduction in your interest payments. Sometimes these capped mortgages have a lower ceiling as well as an upper ceiling.

Lenders are likely to charge a premium for this type of mortgage so borrowers are advised to do their research to compare the rates on offer and the fees.

*Advantages of Capped Mortgages:*

- Enables you to limit your exposure to interest rate increases but also benefit from decreases in interest rates.

- Offers a degree of control over your mortgage payments and makes them less volatile.

*Disadvantages of Capped Mortgages:*

- Lenders can levy high fees for the privilege of having your bread buttered on both sides.

- Penalties are usually payable if you wish to switch or pay off your mortgage within the agreed term.

## Self Certification Mortgage

This type of mortgage is for those who find it difficult to prove how much income they earn – for example, self employed people who don't have regular pay cheques going into their bank accounts.

To get this type of mortgage you don't have to prove how much income you earn, you simply have to state what it is likely to be!

Because of the risk attached to self-certification mortgages, they often have higher interest rates and fees. However if you can put down a larger deposit (more than 25%) the rates may be more competitive and only a little more expensive than a standard mortgage.

However, thanks to the credit crunch, banks have been tightening up their lending criteria for this group of mortgages.

*Advantages of Self Certification Mortgages:*

- Useful for those who cannot get other types of mortgage because they cannot prove how much income they earn.

*Disadvantages of Self Certification Mortgages:*

- Often people are tempted to overstate their income which can make it difficult to keep up payments if interest rates increase.

- The interest rates, deposits and fees are generally higher than other mortgages. Since the credit crunch lenders now view this type of borrower as much higher risk.

## Interest Only Mortgage

These are mortgages where the borrower only pays interest each month but does not make any capital repayments. In simple terms, if a borrower takes a £100,000 interest-only mortgage for 25 years, then after 25 years they will still owe the lender £100,000.

Many buy-to-let investors would not have been able to afford property if they did not have access to interest only mortgages. With rental yields averaging just under 6%, it would be impossible to meet lenders' rental cover requirements with a repayment mortgage.

In fact, many people would not have been able to afford their homes without interest only mortgages. This type of mortgage, along with the ready availability of cheap money, partly explains why house price growth has outstripped wage growth over the last 10 years.

*Advantages of Interest Only Mortgages:*

- Monthly payments are significantly lower than for repayment mortgages.

- The loan doesn't go down over time but eventually, if everything goes to plan, the property should be worth a lot more than the outstanding loan.

- Often the only way for first time buyers to get on the property ladder and keep their mortgage payments affordable.

- Useful for those expecting large financial outlays in the early years, such as school fees.

*Disadvantages of Interest Only Mortgages*

- They're risky! Because you don't pay off any of the mortgage from month to month you're more likely to fall into negative equity when house prices are falling as they are now.

- They're more expensive. You will pay much more interest over the period of the loan because you're always paying interest on the original amount of the loan. With a repayment mortgage, your interest payments decrease as you make capital repayments.

- When interest rates rise, it has a proportionally bigger effect on your monthly payments. Although, by the same token, when interest rates fall there will be a proportionally bigger fall in your monthly payments.

**Repayment Mortgages**

This is the traditional type of mortgage used more by homeowners than buy-to-let investors. A portion of each monthly payment goes towards paying interest and a portion goes towards repaying the loan.

*Advantages of Repayment Mortgages:*

- At the end of the mortgage term you will own the house outright.

- Payments are less volatile to changes in interest rates.

- There are many variations, such as discounted variable rates, and these can be handy if you need to reduce your monthly payments.

*Disadvantages of Repayment Mortgages:*

- In the short term your monthly mortgage payments will be substantially higher because you're making both interest and capital repayments.

- This may be the worst type of mortgage if you are experiencing cash flow problems or are worried about big interest rate increases. The extra money you spend repaying the loan may be better employed building an emergency cash fund.

## Offset Mortgages

In times of economic uncertainty it's a good idea to build a cash reserve to protect yourself from rising mortgage interest rates or even losing your job or business.

An offset mortgage is an extremely tax effective way of doing this – instead of the bank paying you interest on your savings, which is taxed, it will charge you less interest on your mortgage.

Here's an example of why not having to pay interest is much better than earning it:

If you put £1,000 in a savings account and earn 5% interest you could be left with just 3% after the taxman has taken his slice. If instead you take that £1,000 and use it to reduce your mortgage you will save yourself, say, 6% interest.

In other words you pay twice as much interest as you earn on identical sums of money. That's why it's usually better to pay off your mortgage than keep your money in a savings account.

An offset mortgage gives you the best of both worlds – big savings on mortgage interest plus ready access to emergency cash!

*Advantages of Offset Mortgages:*

- They can substantially reduce your mortgage interest payments.

- It gives you flexibility to save or spend money as your circumstances change... ideal during periods of economic uncertainty.

- They're tax efficient because interest on a savings account is normally taxed at up to 40%.

- The interest rate on a mortgage is usually higher than on a savings account. Many current accounts may only pay you 1% but your mortgage interest rate may be over 6%. Therefore it's better not paying interest than earning it.

*Disadvantages of Offset Mortgages:*

- **Most offset mortgages allow the** borrower a certain credit limit in the beginning and if you're not disciplined about paying this back, you could be left with a big loan to pay.

- Offset mortgages sometimes come with higher interest rates so they may not save you much money if you only have small cash reserves.

## Flexible Mortgages

Flexible mortgages are designed to allow people to pay varying amounts of monthly interest. For example, most flexible mortgages allow borrowers to increase their payments, so as to pay off the mortgage early, or to take payment holidays, sometimes for up to six months (although this will mean higher interest payments in the future).

Other features might include the ability to withdraw cash if you've previously made overpayments or reduce your payments during times of financial difficulty.

Flexible mortgages are also known as personal choice mortgages, open plan mortgages and freedom mortgages. They're sometimes combined with other traditional mortgage deals such as:

- Flexible base rate tracker mortgage – this enables you to vary your payments and still benefit from a rate that tracks the Bank of England base rate.

- Flexible discount mortgage - this enables you to vary your payments and enjoy discounts off the standard variable rate.

- Flexible fixed mortgage - with this deal you can vary your payments and have a fixed rate at the same time.

*Advantages of Flexible Mortgages:*

- Suitable for the self employed and others with unpredictable income.

- Useful in times of hardship or financial difficulty.

- If your financial position improves you can save interest by paying off your mortgage early.

*Disadvantages of Flexible Mortgages:*

- Payment holidays or underpayments may lead to further financial problems further down the road.

- Deferring payments will cost you a lot more mortgage interest in the long run.

- If you are not prepared to make overpayments when times are good this is probably not the best solution because you should be able to find a cheaper standard mortgage.

## Mortgage Costs

Since the credit crunch started to bite lenders have dramatically increased the costs they charge for providing mortgages. These include:

- **Arrangement fees**. These are often 'disguised' because lenders add them to the mortgage instead of making you pay them upfront. When property prices were rising strongly most investors shrugged off these costs because they were small compared with the money being made from rising property prices. But with property prices falling, mortgage arrangement fees could eat up a significant amount of the equity in your portfolio if you have to remortgage every couple of years. What's more, you have to pay interest on these fees if they're added onto your mortgage. Arrangement fees range from a few hundred pounds up to 2% of the property's value – I have even come across higher fees!

- **Mortgage indemnity premiums.** The cost of these vary substantially from lender to lender but they all serve the same purpose: to protect the lender against any costs should you default and your property is repossessed. This insurance only protects the lender and not you, the borrower. The fee can sometimes be added to the loan. A useful tip if you are remortgaging is to ask your old lender for a refund of some of the premium charged. You may not get it but it's worth asking!

# CHAPTER 4

# Considering Your Mortgage Strategy

## Putting It All Together

When considering your mortgage strategy going forward it is important to determine:

- Your investment strategy

- Your long-term goals

- The current health of your portfolio

- To what extent you can absorb falling property prices

- To what extent you can absorb rising interest rates

When considering remortgaging think of what types of mortgage will meet your investment goals. If you cannot absorb large increases in interest rates because you are not making sufficient rental profits, you may want to limit your exposure to interest rate increases by having either a capped or fixed-rate mortgage and then focus on improving your portfolio's rental income and reducing operating costs.

There are a few crucial details that every landlord with mortgages needs to keep a close eye on in the current climate:

## When does my fixed rate deal end?

This is extremely important and I use an Excel program to warn me four months in advance when my fixed-rate deals are coming to an end. It's advisable to begin looking for a suitable remortgage at this stage and, if possible, start getting some quotes. These can be kept open for up to three months and if rates increase you are usually able to take up the original quote (however, always check this with the lender). However, if rates go down, you can always get a new quote.

## What standard variable rate (SVR) will apply?

Once a mortgage deal expires the interest rate automatically reverts to the lender's standard variable rate, which could be 2% higher than the Bank of England base rate. Most landlords remortgage at this point. However, if your lender's SVR is not too high (some only charge 0.5%-1% more than the base rate) this may not be worthwhile.

Most borrowers can enjoy a lower monthly payment if they remortgage but will probably have to pay substantial arrangement fees which will add significantly to the overall cost. Arrangement fees have increased by over 100% during the credit crunch.

Lenders have different SVRs so make sure you shop around and consult a suitably qualified mortgage advisor.

## Know your cash flow position over the next year

We've already shown how an investor with 10 properties in his portfolio could go from making a rental profit of £480 per month to a loss of around £1,000 per month if his mortgages reset to a standard variable rate of 7.5%.

Overall the landlord's cash flow has worsened by £1,480 per month – this equates to a loss £17,760 for the year!

There are very few people who are able to sustain a loss of this magnitude for any period of time. That's why I stress that landlords absolutely have to know what their cash position will be over the next 12 months... at least.

The problem, of course, is you don't know what will happen to interest rates. However, it is still possible to look at a few different scenarios using some simple spreadsheets.

Such an exercise will give you a clearer picture of your best and worst case scenarios and enable you to put together a clear plan of action to overcome any substantial monthly shortfalls caused by higher interest rates.

I have included a detailed cash flow analysis near the end of the book which you might find helpful. You can also download it at:
www.taxcafe.co.uk/creditcrunchlinks.html

Bottom line is that landlords need to plan ahead!

## Talk to your lender

Some lenders will let you switch mortgages before your existing deal ends without charging you the full redemption penalties, so call and find out. There will usually be a fee for this, but if the benefits outweigh the costs it may be worth considering.

Some investors whose fixed rate deals have come to an end have been unable to remortgage (because their equity is too low) and have seen their mortgage payments jump by between 25% and 50%.

If you find yourself in this position and raising the rent will still leave you with a shortfall, and you are unable to finance the difference, then you may be in serious financial difficulty.

You may already be running behind on your mortgage payments, or anticipate problems in the near future. Whatever the case, the most important thing to do is speak to your lender.

Mortgage lenders are typically governed by the Financial Services Authority when it comes to recovering mortgages that are in arrears. Make sure you do not ignore any notices – the lender will be following a standard procedure and if they do not hear from you will proceed to repossess the property, a process that will cost you additional fees and penalties.

Lenders like it when you communicate and it is important to give them a realistic indication of the mortgage payments you can afford to make. Apply this logic to your own tenants. If they told you they could not pay the rent anymore you would probably begin eviction proceedings. But if they told you they could afford a certain amount each month, you would possibly be a bit more accommodating and try to find a solution.

Not every lender will be open to this sort of negotiation and some may begin repossession proceedings straight away. However, it is possible to get fixed rate deals re-instated (albeit at higher interest rates) or payment arrangements made for a fixed term. The best thing to do is speak to your lender and ask.

## Measures of Last Resort!

If you're extremely strapped for cash and unable to meet your next mortgage payments you have two measures of last resort:

### 1. Request a Payment Holiday

Those landlords who have never missed a mortgage payment may not even know that lenders offer payment holidays. This allows you to stop making payments for a pre-determined period of time. Different lenders have different criteria: some offer just a one month holiday, while others may offer six months. Additional criteria often apply such as your payment history, the extent of your mortgage arrears and how long you've had the mortgage – many lenders won't consider a payment holiday if the mortgage is less than six months old.

This may sound too good to be true! If you obtain a payment holiday for all of your mortgages you could end up with a significant cash-flow boost.

Applying this to a portfolio of 10 properties with a mortgage of £102,000 per property and a rate of 5.75%, the total saving for 1 month would be £4,888. If you were able to obtain a payment holiday for all your properties for six months you would save £29,325!

This would certainly go a long way towards helping you build up a significant cash reserve to weather the credit crunch. It is imperative, however, that these funds are saved and not spent on non-essential items such as personal holidays. After all, by taking up a payment holiday you are in effect increasing your total mortgage debt which will cost you a significant amount over the life of the mortgage.

I must, however, stress that payment holidays are a VERY expensive option. The lender may charge you a fee and will typically add the payments you've missed onto your mortgage.

So not only will your total debt increase but you will be charged interest on this extra debt!

So only consider this option as a measure of last resort. If you intend selling a property but need help meeting your mortgage because the property is unoccupied, then this option might be suitable. However, if you can't sell the property or the sale falls through, you could run into financial trouble. I would suggest you consult a suitably qualified professional before relying on this option.

## 2. Sell Your Property

If you cannot afford your buy-to-let mortgage and have no other options available then your last resort is to sell the property or have it repossessed. Selling would be the easiest option and it may be best to sell at auction to ensure a quick exchange and completion.

However, if you wish to use an agent it could take anything from one week up to forever to sell the property in the current climate. The average time it takes to sell a property has risen significantly during the credit crunch. You will only get a quick sale if the price is realistic, which means lower than similar properties in your area.

If you decide to sell at auction then typically a buyer will be seen to exchange contracts at the fall of the hammer. They then usually have 28 days to complete so the whole process is quite quick.

It's worth noting, however, that buyers at auction are typically looking for properties that are below market value, hence it is unrealistic to set your reserve price too close to the open market value.

Also it is worth noting that, according to the Essential Information Group, the number of auction lots offered for sale nationally has dropped 10% over the last year, while the percentage sold has dropped 30%.

This is partly due to the lack of affordable finance available but also indicates that buyers expect lower prices and are more choosy. In the current climate it may be impossible to sell your property at the price you would like or need to repay your mortgage.

However, where you have sufficient equity, achieving even a small profit after selling may make this option worthwhile if you are struggling to cover your monthly costs.

# CHAPTER 5

# Your Credit Score

## Keep on Top of Your Credit Score

If you are intending to maintain a property portfolio or perhaps more importantly if you are hoping to expand your portfolio, it is absolutely imperative that you are able to source the most competitive loans available.

One of the most important ways you can do this is by ensuring your credit record is clean. If lenders pick up any irregularities, or anything else that indicates you are a risky borrower, they could quite easily reject your application outright!

Even if you don't receive an outright rejection you may not be able to obtain the best deals available which ultimately will lead to higher finance costs and less money in your pocket!

Your credit report is a key element of your financial CV and details all the credit you have taken out such as credit cards, loans and mortgages, along with your repayment history, any court judgments against you and other information.

Information on your credit report is taken from two main sources - public records and from lenders. The public records hold information such as court judgments and whether you are registered to vote.

Many lenders share details of their customers' credit accounts, such as the amount they have lent and whether repayments are made on time.

Lenders usually check your credit report when you apply for a loan and use this information, along with information on your application form, to assess whether you are likely to repay what you owe on time. This helps them decide whether to make you an offer and what interest rate to charge you.

Lenders will refuse credit for a number of reasons, usually when information held by a credit reference agency leads them to believe that the borrower will have trouble making repayments. It could be that the applicant has failed to make up-to-date repayments in the past or that incorrect information has been given on an application form.

No-one has an absolute right to be granted credit but there are certain rules that apply, for example people cannot be refused simply because of race, gender, religion, sexual orientation or address.

Lenders must give the main reason why you have been refused and whether the refusal is the result of information provided by a credit reference agency. If this is the case you can ask the lender for the relevant details.

## What Your Credit Report Shows

Your report covers all the information you are entitled to under Section 7 of the Data Protection Act 1998, which includes:

- The information you have given about yourself when you previously applied to different lenders for different types of credit.

- Electoral roll information in your name at your present address.

- Financial information, such as county court judgments (CCJs), credit accounts or searches in your name.

- Any previous or forwarding addresses in your name.

- The names of your financial associates: people with whom you share an account, have made a joint application for credit or with whom you have another financial connection.

- Information provided by CIFAS, the UK's Fraud Prevention Service, about your address, such as whether they have ever been used fraudulently.

- Searches by lenders when you apply for credit.

- If your report has been searched by a lender because a financial associate has made an application for credit that will also appear on your credit report.

- Names of other people who live at your address or addresses from the electoral roll.

- Details of people with whom you share a financial connection.

Lenders do not see:

- The names of companies you have accounts with.

- Recorded searches that were made with your consent to confirm your identity but were not part of a credit application.

If you share a financial connection with someone and have recently been refused credit, it may be a good idea for the other person to request a copy of his or her credit report too.

## Improving Your Credit Score

If you would like to improve your credit report you should take note of the following pointers:

- **Understand your credit report.** You need to know what's there and how it affects you before you can make any improvements.

- **Tidy up the details.** If you disagree with anything, contact the relevant lender, explain the problem and ask them to remove or amend the entry.

- **Protect your identity.** If you notice something strange, such as a loan application you didn't make, you could be a victim of identity fraud. Get in touch with the credit report provider to investigate. Experian, for instance, offers victims of fraud services that can help.

- **Register to vote at your current address.** Lenders use the electoral roll to check that you are who you say you are and live where you claim to live, as a precaution against fraud. If you aren't registered or are registered at a previous address, they may ask for proof of your identity and address, or even turn you down.

- **Assert your independence.** Your credit report has a section listing your financial associates – people with whom you share a joint account, such as a mortgage or credit card. When you apply for credit, lenders may also check their credit reports, in case their financial situation makes it difficult for you to repay the loan. So if you're separated or divorced, you should also separate your finances, tell your lenders and let your credit report provider know.

- **Don't leave credit application footprints.** When you are researching new credit deals, make sure that lenders understand you only want information. Every credit application results in a search of your credit report, which leaves a record. If a lender needs to search your credit report before giving you a quote, make sure they do a quotation search which will not be seen by other lenders. If other lenders see lots of these, they may think you are desperate for money or that a fraud is being planned.

- **Cut back on borrowing.** Lenders like to see people who have comfortably managed their repayments over time and aren't struggling to keep up with multiple debts. For example, if you have a lot of credit cards, see if you can pay off a few entirely.

- **Tell the truth at all times.** Don't lie or blur the truth on an application form – it amounts to fraud and could leave a record on your credit report when lenders uncover inaccuracies.

- **Keep on checking your credit report.** Your credit report changes as your circumstances change, so it's important to check it regularly.

- **Don't get behind on payments.** Always make your repayments on time. Never take out more credit to pay interest on existing borrowings – instead, let the lenders know you've got problems and they will help you work out a schedule of payments you can afford. This is extremely important because if you miss payments this will be displayed on your credit report for many years. Below is a summary of the types of repayment problems that lenders can see on your credit report and the length of time that each stays on your report:

- **Court judgments** - six years, although they can be removed if you pay your debt in full within a month of the judgment.

- **Missed repayments** - six years after the date you settle an account.

- **Defaulted accounts** - only removed six years after the date when the account fell into default.

- **Repossessions** - stay on for six years from the repossession date.

- **IVAs and bankruptcies** - recorded for at least six years

There are numerous credit report service providers who allow you to keep up to date with changes to your credit report, including:

- www.experian.co.uk
- www.equifax.co.uk
- www.creditexpert.co.uk

This is important, especially with the proliferation of identity theft, whereby criminals use your personal details to obtain loans which are never repaid and end up harming your credit score. Even though these cases can be resolved your ability to borrow will be severely impaired in the short term.

## Don't Miss a Single Mortgage Payment

Perhaps the cardinal sin for any landlord is to miss a mortgage payment! If this happens this will immediately reflect on your credit score and could affect any future mortgages you apply for. Don't risk it! If you cannot meet any mortgage payments tell the lender beforehand and try to agree a payment holiday or some other payment deal.

## Keep Personal Loan and Credit Card Applications to a Minimum

Many landlords do not realise the impact that their personal lending habits may have on their ability to secure mortgage finance. If you apply for too many personal loans and credit cards over a period of say 12 months, not only does this bring your credit score down substantially, but mortgage lenders take those as proof that you are not financially responsible and could refuse to lend to you.

With the mortgage market having contracted so much over the last six months, it is not advisable to restrict the number of lenders who will lend to you because you have poor personal finances.

## Don't Miss any Personal Loan Payments

Just as important as not missing mortgage payments is to not miss any payments for personal loans or personal accounts such as credit cards, store cards, or services. If this is reflected on your credit report it will bring down your score and also indicate to lenders that you are financially irresponsible.

# CHAPTER 6

# Rental Income Strategies

R ent is the lifeblood of a property portfolio. Without it you are unable to service your mortgages and pay your other operating costs. There are many aspects to getting your rental strategy right, such as: constantly reviewing existing rents to ensure they are competitive (not too high or too low), trying to continually increase rents to improve cash flow and profits and reducing the risk of rental voids. Let's take a closer look at the key components of your rental strategy.

## Is the Rent I Am Asking for Competitive?

It may seem like a silly question, however, it is the most important one of all. Rents are equivalent to the sales of a business – without them there is no business!

Similarly, would you be happy to sell someone something for less than you know they would pay? I have come across many landlords who have not had an accurate assessment of their properties' rental potential.

There are many reasons for this:

- A landlord may have been quoted a rent far in excess of what's realistic by a letting agent trying to attract business. As a result the property sits empty.

- A landlord may have been quoted a rent far below what's realistic by a letting agent trying to secure a quick commission.

- A landlord may not have looked at enough comparables before setting the rent. This can result in the rent being set too high or too low.

- A tenant may have been in a property for a number of years and as a result rents have not been increased sufficiently.

Whatever the reason, it is imperative to look at your rents at least twice a year.

*I recently did this exercise and was able to increase my rents by 10% on 7 properties!*

There are obviously guidelines that need to be followed, for example notices need to be served giving sufficient warning (typically 2 months). Your existing tenancy agreements may not allow rent reviews to take place. Landlords are not allowed to simply increase rents as and when they like so ensure you take advice from a suitable professional before serving rent increase notices.

## Am I Maximising Rental Yields?

Besides just trying to increase rents, it's also important to ensure you are using each of your properties to its full potential.

For example, a four-bedroom house may rent for £900 a month to a single family, however, by properly researching the market in the area, you can assess whether there is scope to rent rooms out on an individual basis.

If you are able to achieve £80 per week per room for the four-bed house, you will end up earning rental income of £1,387 – a 54% increase.

However, before doing this there are various factors to consider:

- Room rentals are a lot more work. Tenant turnover tends to be much higher, as are advertising costs to source new tenants. There will be more tenant screenings and viewings, billing for services (gas, electricity, water and council tax) can get tricky and where included in the room rate can eat up profits substantially, maintenance & repair costs are typically higher than single family homes.

- Initial investment is higher – typically furniture and communal appliances and equipment will need to be provided, rooms will need to be fitted with individual locks. Furniture and linen has to comply with relevant fire regulations, so make sure you investigate this.

- Homes in Multiple Occupancy (HMO) regulations may apply in which case a licence from your local council will need to be obtained which involves various checks and compliance issues – a call to your local council will clarify this.

- If your property is mortgaged the lender may have imposed restrictive clauses preventing the property from being used as an HMO.

- Buildings and contents insurance costs may be higher.

## Can I Increase My Rents?

If you have found a tenant at a competitive rent it is still possible and highly recommended to pursue a higher rent at the end of the tenancy term. I tend to sign tenants up for six-month Assured Shorthold Tenancies (AST). This way I have the option of increasing rents twice every twelve months.

Once again the relevant guidelines need to be followed, however there have been various instances where I have been able to pass on rent increases to a tenant just by having an open relationship with them and explaining my reasons. These include:

- My mortgage rate has recently increased and unfortunately I have to ask you for more rent.

- I have spoken to a lettings agent in the area and they have just let a property on this street for £X a month more.

- I have spoken to a lettings agent in the area and they have told me they have desperate tenants wanting similar properties to mine at £X a month more than you are paying.

It is even possible to ask for an increase if you are providing your tenants with certain extras. For instance, I have on many occasions been able to increase the rent initially asked for by providing tenants with appliances, white goods, or furniture.

Getting an additional £25 a month is easy if the tenant feels they are getting something for it – just make sure you don't over spend as you could be unnecessarily increasing your risk.

I have heard of landlords providing the full quota of goods (fridge, washer/dryer, microwave, beds etc) only to see the tenants disappear after three months. Good tenant vetting can eliminate these types of surprises, however.

It's important to add that with rising inflation affecting many tenants, there are limits to how much extra rent they can absorb. Utility bills are expected to increase 40%, food price inflation is in double digits and oil prices and transport costs are rising rapidly.

All this means less disposable income for tenants which will put even more pressure on their ability to meet existing rents. It's likely many tenants will downgrade to cheaper properties and this in turn will improve rental yields for cheaper types of property as more people compete for a static supply of properties in this bracket.

## Switch from Monthly to Weekly Rent

This is one of those examples that illustrates how a little change can have a big impact. Many landlords advertise a monthly rate, for example £500 per month. This equates to an annual rent of £6,000.

Now if you were to divide this same £500 a month rent by 4 weeks, this comes to £125 a week. Multiply this by the number of weeks in the year (52 weeks) and you end up with £6,500. That's an additional month's rent!

Now most people will realise that there are typically more than 4 weeks per month. The exact answer is 4.33 weeks (52 weeks / 12 months = 4.33 weeks per month). Hence the correct weekly charge should be £115.47 per week (£500/4.33).

Although £125 a week is not a lot more than £115, in cases where you can get away with advertising a weekly rent, most tenants will calculate the monthly figure by multiplying by four and you could end up with an extra month's rent.

It is important, however, that you ensure the rent you're asking for is competitive, and never attempt to trick a tenant into thinking they are paying less than they are. For instance, if you are asking for £500 a month, and switch to weekly rents, you must charge your tenant £115.57 a week, not £125!

Ultimately, the market in your area will dictate the payment method. If all properties are advertised with monthly rents you may be inclined to stick to this. However, it is still worth testing the water.

There is a slight drawback to earning weekly rents – instead of receiving £500 at the beginning of each month and earning interest on the whole amount for the whole month, the rent will be received in weekly increments and some interest will be lost. However, this will be significantly less than what you stand to gain.

## Other Ways of Improving Rent

One of the easiest ways of increasing your rental income is by having more tenants in each property. This is not the same as having an HMO where a set of strangers live together and share communal areas and appliances.

I have had instances where a three-bedroom house has been let to a family who are not using the third bedroom. In some cases, tenants have approached me and asked if they can move a work colleague or family member, such as a brother or sister, into the spare room.

In other cases I have approached tenants who I know are receptive to providing accommodation to professionals seeking rooms. Whatever the case, this represents an ideal opportunity to improve your rent received. I typically ask for an additional £70 per week for a double room, or £50 per week for a single room. This equates to en extra £3,640 or £2,600 respectively for virtually no additional outlay or work.

Considering a portfolio of 10 properties if you apply this to just 1 property, you will improve your Portfolio Rental Figure (PRF) by between 4.3% and 6.1%. This will obviously vary depending on the area where your properties are located, the demand for room rentals, the type of tenants you have etc. If your tenant is uncertain as to whether they would be happy with this arrangement, you can perhaps agree that they receive a small reduction in their rent.

It is worth noting that you should pursue advice from a suitably qualified professional to confirm the exact way in which your tenancy agreement would need to be altered to account for the additional rent (it is best to maintain tenancies on just one tenancy, rather than having multiple tenancies).

Also, if you have a mortgage, the lender may impose restrictions on this type of letting arrangement although by staying with one tenancy agreement this can be overcome. It would be best to confirm with your lender if you're unsure.

## Rent Increases: Importance to Long-term Portfolio Health

Besides the immediate cash flow benefit of obtaining a higher rent, there is a much more important reason why you should adopt a strategy of regular rent increases.

I accept that in instances where rents are depressed because of economic circumstances, or localized reasons, such as a major employer shutting a factory, it will be difficult to push through any increases.

*Figure 5. How Your Rental Income Can Grow*

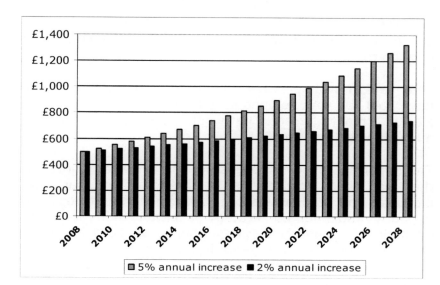

However, with the number of property buyers lower than ever, and the number of tenants higher than ever, this has generally been pushing up rental yields, as more people compete for the same number of properties (remember major house builders have stopped new building projects because they cannot sell new units).

Figure 5 illustrates two rental increase scenarios:

Starting with a monthly rent of £500 in 2008:

- With a 5% per annum rent increase, by 2018 you will be receiving £815 a per month and by 2028 you will be receiving £1,327 per month!

- With a 2% per annum rent increase, by 2018 you will be receiving £609 per month and by 2028, £743 per month.

Part of the reason for the difference is the effect of compound interest. I accept that unless inflation, wage increases and a shortage of housing persist until 2028, it is difficult to imagine someone paying twice as much rent as they do today.

That said, I wonder what my great grandmother would have said if I told her people pay me between £500 and £1,000 a month in rent. That would have been the price of a house when she was 20!

The important thing to note is not the actual amounts but the fact that a disciplined strategy of regular rent increases can reap substantial rewards in the future. Even a poorly implemented strategy is better than none. An example of a poor strategy is when a landlord increases rent every two or three years in reaction to either seeing competitor landlords properties, or being advised to do so by letting agents.

For every month that goes by that you charge a lower than achievable rent, you forfeit future profits.

I have viewed countless properties where landlords (including 'experienced' landlords with substantial portfolios) were charging rents up to 25% below what could be achieved, often because they have long standing tenants. But in the existing economic and financial climate, giving away 25% of your rent because you're too lazy to find a new tenant is a recipe for disaster.

So bottom line for landlords is: always try to keep upward pressure on your rents and keep your eyes open to what competitor landlords are charging!


## Void Periods

The dirty word in property has to be voids. There's nothing worse than having a property sitting empty, especially if you have a mortgage and it's costing you money.

The best way to avoid having empty properties is to make sure you know exactly when tenancies are coming to an end and take action. It's easy for a landlord to assume that a long-term or reliable tenant will renew. However, the onus is on you to find out whether they do in fact intend to stay in the property.

Most assured short hold tenancies contain a clause which requires the tenant to give minimum notice (typically 28 days) of their intention to terminate the agreement. Many landlords rely on this and assume that if no notice is given the tenant will be staying on. However, this can often lead to problems and ultimately additional costs.

I make sure I know when each and every one of my tenancy agreements is up for renewal and always remind the tenant of their obligation to provide me with the required notice. In virtually all cases I am given confirmation by the tenant of their intention to terminate or extend their tenancy agreement.

Many landlords use software programs which allow them to track the end of tenancies. Alternatively, you can use a simple Excel spreadsheet like the one I use (see Figure 6).

The purpose of this spreadsheet is to provide a quick snapshot of your portfolio, including information as to when tenancies are up for renewal and to ensure that notices are served in the correct timeframe. Many landlords wait until the tenancy is just about to expire before asking tenants whether they will be staying on. The net effect is properties become empty and voids eat into your rental profits.

A property is most likely to lie empty immediately after it has been purchased. This may be because it requires repairs or because the landlord was uncertain about the completion date and did not advertise for tenants.

*Figure 6. Spreadsheet Warning of Lease Expiring*

**Property number**

| | 1 | PROPERTY ADDRESS |
|---|---|---|
| | | COMPLETED 12-07-2006 |
| Current Lender: | Mortgage Express - Tel: 0800 000 000 |
| | A/c No: ABCDEFGHIJK |

Mortgage amount = £102,000, interest rate = 5.39%
till 01/01/200X, 5% redemption penalty - variable rate 7%
as of 01/01/200X

| TENANCY DETAILS | May-08 | Jun-08 | Jul-08 | Aug-08 | Sep-08 | Oct-08 | Nov-08 | Dec-08 |
|---|---|---|---|---|---|---|---|---|
| Rental Received | 575 | 575 | 575 | 575 | Lease begins - 01-05-2008 ends 01/05/09 - 2 month notice - £750 deposit held by Landlord | | | |
| Service Charge Payment | | | | | | | | |
| Mortgage Payment | 458.15 | 458.15 | 458.15 | 458.15 | | | | |
| Agents Commission Paid | | | | | | | | |
| Buildings Insurance | 10 | 10 | 10 | 10 | | | | |
| Council Tax | | | | | | | | |
| Repairs & Maintenance | | | | 60 new Corgi Cert | | | | |
| Key Events | CORGI CERT RENEW 01/08/09 | | | | MORTAGE TERM ENDING 01/01/2009 | | | |

To access a downloadable working copy of this spreadsheet please visit: www.taxcafe.co.uk/creditcrunchlinks.html

Things you can do to minimize this type of void include:

- Agreeing a completion date upon exchange of contracts and arranging with the vendor to allow you access to show prospective tenants around the property before the completion date.

- Providing prospective tenants with a list of the work to be carried out and a timeframe. You could agree an initial reduction in rent while the work is carried out.

- Where a property will have to be left empty while repairs are carried out, it is advisable to get quotes between the exchange and completion dates. You don't want to be waiting for quotes after you have completed.

## Reduce Void Periods

### 1. Two month notice period to terminate tenancy

One very useful tip to help alleviate the occurrence of voids is to change your tenancy agreement to stipulate that the tenant must give 2 months notice of their intention to leave – two months is normally more than enough time to find new tenants.

It's worth noting that, although you may include a two month notice period in the agreement, it is unlikely that it would be legally enforceable.

However, tenants typically accept what's in the tenancy agreement and it is unlikely that most would bother challenging such a clause. Before you do this, however, I would recommend taking advice from a suitably qualified professional.

## 2. Chase late rent payments aggressively

If you do not chase rents or frequently tolerate late payment you are sending your tenants a clear message that you are weak and it's okay to mess you around.

If you fall behind with your mortgage payments, your lender will send out urgent letters. Why would you expect things to be different between a tenant and landlord?

Once arrears have been built up, they're usually difficult to clear. If arrears grow to the point where they exceed the deposit held by the landlord, tenants are often tempted to vacate the property without notice. This happened to a landlord I know and the tenants also trashed his property.

Understandably tenants do sometimes experience difficulty due to factors beyond their control, for example if they're made redundant or fall ill. However, it's important to maintain pressure and if possible obtain guarantors. This way you can claim from the guarantor should the tenant default.

In rare instances tenants may not have a suitable guarantor and may be unable to pay any rent owing. Typically you then have to issue the relevant notice requiring re-possession of the property.

I had such an instance with a tenant who had become unemployed and could not find a new job. He was married and had just had twins. He was located quite close to a number of my other properties, some of which required minor maintenance such as internal painting, minor building work and garden clean ups.

After speaking to the tenant I discovered that he was quite skilled at DIY, so I offered to pay him a daily rate to work on my other properties. Not only did I get the work done at a fraction of what other contractors would have charged, he also managed to clear his outstanding rent which meant he stayed in the property. He is now one of my best tenants!

## 3. Marketing to the right tenants using the right tools

I see so many examples of landlords using the wrong marketing techniques to attract tenants. If you have a property in a relatively poor area, putting it on the internet is not the best way to attract your target market. Neither is advertising your swanky bachelor pad in the classifieds.

I've made sure I know the best methods for each of my properties, to the extent that I have the relevant newspapers, websites and council contacts to use when I need to find new tenants.

To illustrate, I used to place adverts for property to rent in a Northamptonshire town. I used to get one or two responses a week, and between using this and various lettings agents, I ended up with roughly one void month per property per year – I have 15 properties in this area, so this was making a big dent in my rental profits!

I ended up getting a few Housing Benefit tenants in place and by taking large deposits, having guarantors and checking previous landlord and employment references I was able to get good quality tenants.

I then decided to approach the local council and gave my details as a private landlord offering quality accommodation to tenants on Housing Benefits. The response has been great ever since and I typically have three or four tenants competing for my properties. I don't end up with void periods, I get rents more than 20% higher than other private landlords who don't accept DSS tenants, and I hold double the deposit from these tenants.

The point I'm trying to make is that if you are accepting void periods as a given you are not marketing your property effectively. You should have tenants queuing up to move into your property. Eliminating void periods can have a dramatic effect on your portfolio's health.

This leads me to the next important point:

## 4. Consider accepting Housing Benefit claimants (DSS)

Many landlords will refuse to deal with tenants claiming housing benefits.

DSS Tenants claim their benefits from their local council and where changes in circumstances, or information requested by the council from the tenant is not provided, the council will typically suspend the tenant's housing benefits payments.

Where benefits are suspended the landlord is not always informed and rental arrears can quickly accumulate.

Although the benefits system can be extremely frustrating and data protection can mean you are left in the dark as to why a benefit award has been suspended, the yields achievable from DSS tenants can often be significantly higher than for ordinary private tenants.

Nevertheless many adverts I see strictly exclude DSS tenants. Some of the reasons for this include:

- DSS tenants would not ordinarily pass credit checks. Landlords who subscribe to rent insurance services, which guarantee rents for tenants that pass credit tests, would then not be covered for these properties.

- Many buy-to-let mortgage agreements specifically state that you cannot rent the property to DSS tenants.

- The housing benefits system has recently changed – councils now *have* to pay tenants their housing benefit directly, unless the tenant is disabled or financially incompetent (8 or more weeks behind on the rent).

- Housing benefit payments are typically paid one month in arrears, so instead of receiving the rent at the beginning of each rental month, it will be received at the end.

- The Data Protection Act prevents council employees from discussing claims with anyone other than the tenant. Also, when there is a change in circumstances which suspends or reduces the amount of the claim, the landlord is the last to find out.

- DSS tenancies can lead to a lot more admin and work because there are two other parties involved (the council and the tenant) and they act independently of each other, often with little feedback to the landlord.

However, there are a number of good reasons why it is still an attractive option to consider letting to DSS tenants, if your properties are in the correct area.

DSS tenants need to go through their local council to qualify for housing benefit.

I have registered my properties with various councils and get many calls each week. When properties are not available, I store details and have tenants on a waiting list.

The following are my tips for reducing problems with DSS tenants:

- Check if the applicant has at least 2 months deposit to lodge – it is possible to get higher deposits, just gauge the tenant's response when you ask. If the tenant queries this request, explain that council payments are usually 4 weeks in arrears and that benefit claim issues can lead to 8 weeks rent arrears, as the council usually delays informing the landlord of any changes in the benefit award.

- Ask for the first month's rent upfront – this way the council has time to process the claim.

- Ensure the tenant has a guarantor who will sign to stand liable for any outstanding rent or damages claim at the end of the tenancy.

- Ensure the identity of the guarantor is verified, using a utility bill, and get an independent person to witness the signatures of both tenants and guarantors on the AST and Guarantor Agreement (GA).

- Run a credit check on the guarantor to determine if they are suitable.

- Make sure the tenant indicates on the initial housing benefit claim form that you, the landlord, are entitled to discuss the claim with the council for the next 12 months, not just once off.

- Always get the tenant to sign an Authority to Disclose form which will entitle the council to discuss all relevant details of the claim with the Landlord. The council should also be required to inform you of any changes to the claim resulting in suspension or reduction in the benefit amount.

- As you will always be running 4 weeks in arrears on the rent, if you do ever reach 8 weeks in arrears ensure you issue the relevant section 21 notice to the tenant to cover yourself and limit your potential rental loss. I would advise consulting a suitably qualified professional to carry out the correct serving of notice procedure.

- Find a contact in the relevant council housing benefit department and build a relationship with that person. Sending update emails once a month will help ensure open communication should the tenant's circumstances change.

- Make sure you set your rent at the right level. If similar properties to your's in the area rent for, say £500, it is perfectly plausible to achieve £550, with the council paying, say, £515, and the tenant paying the shortfall of £35.

- Make sure you quote the rent at a weekly rate. If you use a monthly rate of, say, £500, the council would calculate this as being £115.38 per week. Councils typically pay every 4 weeks so you would only receive £461.53 which is almost 10% less than you might have expected. Although you receive the same yearly amount (£6,000), you only receive the final top up at the end of the year!

So if you expect to achieve £500 per month, ask for £125 per week! It is important, however, to declare your annual rent as £6,500, which converted into months is £541.67. This may mean that you end up with a substantially higher rental than similar properties in the area. However, if you can achieve the higher rent, ask for it.

It is worth noting however, that councils do have methods of calculating a fair and reasonable rent and if the rent is too high the tenant will be required to subsidise the shortfall, which they may not be in a position to do. So try to get a fair rent figure at the beginning of the housing benefit application process.

I know of numerous landlords who cater for DSS tenants and are able to enjoy substantially higher deposits, along with up to 20% higher rents in certain cases. The risks are higher but if managed effectively the rewards can be substantial.

Considering the overall economic climate, it is also likely that more people will be forced to claim housing benefit. As unemployment increases so the demand for DSS housing will increase. This will only serve to further increase the yields available within this sector.

## 5. Problem rentals – Just cannot attract a tenant

Sometimes properties just cannot seem to attract tenants for reasons such as:

- The property is in a severe state of disrepair

- The property is an undesirable area

- There is no tenant demand in the area

There could be lots of other reasons why the property is failing to rent but the solution will fall within one of a few areas. Before mentioning these, it's worth discussing the current economic climate because this should ultimately increase demand for rental property.

Unemployment is expected to increase as businesses struggle to cope with the credit crunch and the effect of inflation on their costs.

Already large numbers of businesses are scaling back operations. For example, many house builders have halted new building work and this will have a ripple effect on contractors and other businesses. Estate agencies are shutting down throughout the country as the shortage of mortgages is crippling the housing market. Already house sales are down by almost 50% from their peak.

Banks are being forced to cut jobs to recoup their losses from bad sub-prime related investments.

Many people cannot afford to buy houses as they are being priced out the market by lenders increasingly toughening their lending criteria, for example by raising minimum deposits.

Repossessions are expected to jump this year, as indicated by the number of lenders reporting an increase in mortgage arrears.

All this points to an increase in demand for rented property. This brings me to the first solution to finding tenants for undesirable properties:

*There is always a tenant willing to rent a property, at the right price. Many landlords are, to put it bluntly, lazy when it comes to finding tenants. There are more tenants than ever before, all you have to do is find one!*

I know a landlord who had a property in a severe state of disrepair. The roof was leaking, walls were cracking, and windows were broken. He could not afford the cost of a full refurbishment but felt there was an opportunity to let it. I thought he was crazy, however, he managed to find a builder who agreed to live in the property while bringing it up to a habitable state. He met the builder by chance in a pub and after finding out he was out of a job and a house, managed to find a mutually beneficial solution.

A year later the property was almost complete and all he had to pay for were some building materials and hiring some equipment. This is an extreme example, however, it illustrates the point that no property is unrentable!

Also make sure you are targeting the right tenants and think about how they would look for your property. Also check whether you are being too restrictive with the tenants you are looking for. I have read adverts saying: No DSS, no students, no pets, no children, no smokers etc. Taken together this excludes a large percentage of the population.

I would be less specific and if an otherwise suitable tenant has a pet or smokes, I see this as an opportunity to perhaps ask for a higher deposit to cover increased repair and maintenance costs or even a higher rent.

You will be surprised just how many prospective tenants in this position will accept these terms, as they are typically excluded by many landlords. Be aware, however, that your repair costs may increase significantly.

## 6. Are you asking for too much rent?

Many landlords will set their rent to cover their mortgage (especially new buy-to-let investors who have bought a property off-plan or new). The risk is that by asking for just £25 a month too much, your property will lie empty and not earn you anything. I prefer to get a tenant into a newly purchased property as soon as possible, even if this means accepting a lower rent. Once a tenant is in, it is easy to push up rents after the first tenancy period comes to an end.

## 7. Does the property need essential repairs/ maintenance?

The last possible resort is to refurbish the property. This may be necessary to bring it to a habitable state (assuming you have not found any homeless unemployed builders in your local pub). If after the refurbishment you still cannot find a tenant then you may be better off selling the property and returning to your day job!

# CHAPTER 7

# Deposits

Typical deposits from tenants are four to six weeks rent and agents and landlords are usually expected to pay the deposit back at the end of the tenancy.

I am surprised how many landlords either do not ask for a deposit or take a very small one. In effect they're exposing themselves to additional risk if the tenant goes into arrears or damages the property.

I aim to achieve at least a 6 week deposit and, where possible, an 8 week deposit.

Where a tenant is required to vacate the property, it is usually a requirement that two months notice is given to allow the tenant to find alternative accommodation.

I would recommend seeking professional advice when recovering possession of a property. Where the reason is rental arrears, notices are usually issued when rental payments are already at least 8 weeks in arrears. If the notice then gives the tenant another two months to vacate the property, the landlord is at risk of losing a total of 16 weeks rent!

Given the current climate of high mortgage interest rates and increasing operating costs, it is highly unlikely that many landlords can afford to lose 16 weeks of rent on just one property, let alone a number of properties in a portfolio.

This is why deposits are such important tools for landlords. It is imperative that, not only is a sufficient deposit taken, but also that it is effectively protected! Below are some ideas on how to achieve both these goals.

## Sign Up to a Tenancy Deposit Scheme

The Government introduced legislation effective since 6th April 2007 which requires that all deposits handled by agents and landlords be protected under a Government approved scheme.

There are two main schemes, the first is an insurance-based scheme specifically designed to enable landlords and agents to hold deposits themselves. The second is a custodial scheme requiring the landlord to hand over the deposit to the scheme administrator. The Government has awarded contracts to three companies to run tenancy deposit schemes.

There are two insurance based schemes and one custodial-based scheme:

- **Tenancy Deposit Solutions Ltd (TDSL) – mydeposits.co.uk**. This insurance-based scheme has a small initial joining fee (currently £58.75) and a deposit protection fee of £30 per tenancy deposit held. It is possible to re-coup this cost from the tenant through a fee charged to cover costs of credit checks, providing tenancy and inventory documents, and the deposit protection. There are also discounts available for members of the National Landlords Association and Residential Landlords Association. The scheme offers a free and impartial dispute resolution service.

- **The Tenancy Deposit Scheme (TDS) – thedisputeservice.co.uk.** This insurance-based scheme was established under the Housing Act 2004 and requires landlords to register details of the start and end of all Assured Shorthold Tenancies for which they take a deposit. This scheme, like the TDSL, was set up to provide three main services, namely: 1) to protect deposits through the tenancy, 2) to ensure the return of the deposit promptly at the end of the tenancy, where there is no dispute and 3) when there is a dispute, to ensure it is dealt with fairly and quickly by the independent complaints examiner.

- **The Deposit Protection Service (DPS) – depositprotection.com.** This service is the only custodial deposit protection scheme and is free to use and open to all landlords and letting agents. The service is funded entirely from the interest earned from deposits held. Landlords and letting agents will be able to register and make transactions online, however, paper forms are also available if required.

I would recommend taking a look at all three schemes in detail before deciding which one to join.

## Am I Asking for Enough Deposit?

It is vital to have at least 2 months deposit from 'risky' tenants. I will discuss ways of reducing the risk of accepting 'risky' tenants through an effective tenant screening process later in the guide. It is even possible to increase deposits held from 1 month to 6 weeks or 8 weeks, if the tenant has requested any items such as appliances or furniture.

Whatever the case, by increasing the deposit held, you are reducing your risk of losses arising from damages and rental arrears.

Assuming a portfolio of 10 properties, increasing the deposits from 1 month's rent to 2 months rent will mean a total of £10,000 will be held, which can offer serious cash flow benefits and a comfortable pool of resources to avoid losses from rent arrears and damages.

## Inventories – The Key to Effective Deposit Protection

I know many landlords who do not carry out inventory inspections when a tenant takes possession of a property. This is one of the biggest mistakes that can be made – without an accurate inventory you are not able to identify if the tenant has in fact damaged anything.

The inventory is the only way of getting your tenant to look after your property properly.

Would you hand over the keys to a £100,000 Ferrari to anyone without making sure the car was checked before and after? Similarly, with buy-to-let properties an inventory should be carried out before a tenant moves into a property and as soon as the tenant vacates the property.

I have saved thousands of pounds by having effective inventories carried out before and after each tenancy. It is very difficult to recover any repair costs from tenants once you've refunded their deposits.

## A Unique Form of Deposit Protection

An interesting service available from Tenantdeposit.com offers an insurance alternative to cash deposits.

If a tenant cannot afford the deposit, rather than lose the tenant, you can get an insurance guarantee put in place which the tenant pays. So if your tenant can only afford a £500 deposit but you want closer to £1,000, you could accept the £500 to cover any outstanding rent and then ask the tenant to take out insurance for the remaining £500.

The initial premium would be around £38 and £12.50 per month thereafter. If for any reason you need to claim any portion of this deposit, Tenantdeposit.com will pay the money to you (assuming you have sufficient proof that the tenant is liable), and they will then pursue the tenant for this amount.

It is important to note that this insurance guarantee does not cover any claims relating to unpaid rent – it only covers damage to a property and its contents.

The tenant typically has to be working, which will exclude certain housing benefit claimants and the tenant's identity has to be verified via a passport and payslip or bank statement.

# CHAPTER 8

# Operating Costs

Running a portfolio of properties can be an expensive business. I am sure that after reading this chapter you will be able to reduce your operating costs at many different levels and ultimately this will help protect you and your portfolio in the current climate of uncertainty.

## Using Letting Agents – Potential Savings

Many buy-to-let investors find it necessary to use a letting agent. For example, you may not have time to find prospective tenants due to work commitments or you may live too far from the property. In these instances, having a reliable letting agent who is proactive when repairs and maintenance are required and diligently collects the rent, is invaluable. This, however, comes at a price!

If you are a serious landlord there are significant financial benefits to self management. Some investors would argue that they can make more money by sticking to what they are good at, for example sourcing properties. However, with the increase in mortgage interest rates and inflation pushing up other costs, this is one key area where you can achieve a major improvement in your portfolio's cash flow.

## Reducing Management Charges

Letting agents charge on average 10% of your rental income. Some charge as much as 15% and some add VAT on top!

If you have to use a letting agent, negotiate a better rate. Threaten them with switching to another agent or tell them you have other properties they could manage.

It's a worthwhile exercise to get quotes from other letting agents in the area and present these to your existing agent. When getting these quotes it's always handy to mention you have a portfolio of properties in the area that you are considering switching to a new company.

The prospect of managing a portfolio rather than a single property will usually encourage the letting agent to offer a more competitive rate.


## Application / Set-up Fees

Many letting agents charge an application fee which will range from £50 up to £250, depending on the area and letting agent. In most cases, just asking for this fee to be dropped will be sufficient. If not, then indicate your dissatisfaction at potentially having to pay the fee for each property in your portfolio. You may get away with having to pay just one fee.


## Renewal Charges

Many agents charge a fee if the tenant renews the lease. In cases where you have used a letting agent just to find you a tenant, and not on a full management basis, you would typically pay a finder's fee which can range from between 2 and 6 weeks rent.

The renewal charge may be smaller than the initial finder's fee but I have never paid and never intend to pay a renewal charge. If an agent finds you a tenant, you should not have to pay them again should they renew. I argue that it is unfair to be paid twice for the same job, especially when there is no extra work for the agent.

## Tenants Deposits

As discussed earlier, by signing up to a tenancy deposit scheme, a landlord can build up a substantial cash reserve.

Letting agents will typically assume that they will hold the deposit on behalf of the tenant. However, you are quite within your rights to request that the deposit be handed to you.

Normally, all the agent will request is a certificate proving your affiliation with the relevant tenancy deposit scheme, and the tenant would require proof that the deposit has been registered with a scheme and is protected.

## Inventories and Tenancy Agreements

Agents will typically charge for an inventory to be carried out, as well as for the provision of a tenancy agreement. There is scope to receive a reduction in the inventory charge if the agent himself carries out the inventory.

However, if the agent utilises a specialist contractor then the fees will be set and unlikely to be reduced. Whoever carries out the inventory should also include digital pictures – the more the better, as any challenge by the tenants will need to be defended with an accurate inventory and, in most cases, pictures.

A poor inventory can ultimately cost you dear because you will be unable to prove damage has been caused by the tenant. Any defects such as marks on walls, carpets, cracks, paint defects, ceilings etc need to be noted and pictured.

Even those items that are working need to be noted as working. A window handle or lock damaged by a tenant will often only get noticed by the next tenant and by then it's too late.

I use a digital camera which I use to take both pictures and video. The more evidence there is to support a claim of damage the better and if your tenant wishes to challenge your claim, you will need as much proof as possible should you end up in front of an Independent Complaints Examiner (if the deposit is protected by one of the tenancy deposit schemes) or other adjudication method.

Also, electrical fittings, plugs, door handles, kitchen handles, cupboards, tiles, taps, basins, toilet roll holders, towel holders, skirting boards, garden tiles etc should have their condition recorded.

**Over the course of time small repairs that are not recognized will add up to be a significant cost!**

To view and freely download a typical inventory form that I use go to www.taxcafe.co.uk/creditcrunchlinks.html

I make notes of the quantities of all items listed, as well as the state of each item and list any defects or damages upfront, accompanied with many digital pictures and even a video of the property.

This may seem a little tedious but has saved me a lot of money by bringing to my attention defects and damages that I ordinarily would not have picked up.

As for tenancy agreements, most agents will charge you for the privilege of utilising their agreement and will likely say it is a proven agreement that has been checked by a solicitor and will hold up in court. This may be true, however, there are many online resources which enable you to obtain tenancy agreements for a fraction of what some agents charge!

For a Free AST please visit:
www.taxcafe.co.uk/creditcrunchlinks.html

## Advantages of Not Using Letting Agents

The following are the potential benefits of **not** using a letting agent:

### 1. Savings through not paying finder's fee commission or full management charges

The typical finder's fee charged by letting agents varies from £250 up to £1,000 per property (excluding VAT), depending on the amount of rent you are looking for and the type of property. The typical management charge is 10% (excluding VAT).

To illustrate potential savings of not using an agent, consider a landlord with a portfolio of 10 properties each renting for £500 a month. If a letting agent is used to find tenants for all 10 properties and only 50% renew, a total of 15 new tenancies would be signed up during the year.

If the agent charges a typical ½ month's rent plus VAT in finder's fees, that comes to £4,406 per year. If the agent fully manages the properties this would cost you £7,050 a year, assuming a 10% management fee plus VAT.

Given the total rent received from all the properties is £60,000 (assuming no voids) the fees are 7.34% for finder's fees and 11.75% for full management.

That's a lot of money that you could use to offset your other costs such as an increase in your mortgage interest.

If you also consider that full management generally includes rent collection, you are effectively paying for a service that is not entirely necessary as most rent payments can be automated through standing orders arranged by the tenant. Unless a tenant has a requirement to pay in cash, rent collection is a relatively mundane service to have to pay for.

## 2. Inventory charges

Most lettings agents will charge a fee for conducting an inventory. Inventory costs typically range from free (in rare cases) up to £200 (exc. VAT).

Assuming an average cost of £100 and the same 10 property portfolio with 15 renewals throughout the year, the total cost including VAT is £1,763, which equates to 2.94% of the portfolio's rental income for the year.

## 3. Tenancy agreement charges

Agents also sometimes charge to provide a tenancy agreement. This can once again range from being free up to £100 (excluding VAT). Some agents also charge additional set-up fees of up to £200. In total these additional charges can be substantial over a year and across your whole property portfolio.

Applying this to the same portfolio of 10 properties and using an average tenancy agreement charge of £100, 15 tenancy renewals will cost £1,763 (inc. VAT) which is 2.94% of the portfolio's rental income for the year.

## 4. Void periods

If your property sits empty the only person who loses money is YOU! Letting agents will not feel the same pain as a landlord with a big mortgage to pay. My experience with using agents is that I can typically expect a one month void period for each of my properties.

Assuming the same portfolio of 10 properties, the loss from voids would be £6,000 per year, which is 10% of the portfolio rental figure. Given that this is the second largest impact on the portfolio rental figure, it is essential to ensure voids are kept to a minimum. If you use a letting agent you have much less control over this key factor.

## 5. Maintenance / Repairs

Some letting agents make money out of you from repairs and maintenance. It is not uncommon for agents to add their own mark-up to repair bills with agreement from the contractor. These can be anywhere from 5% up to 20%. I would prefer to remain in control of this cost. If the average repair and maintenance cost without using an agent is £350 (inc VAT) per property per year, this means that using agents I can expect my repair bill to increase by £525 per year if the agent adds a 15% mark-up. This represents just under 1% of the portfolio's rental income.

## 6. Charge tenants an admin fee to cover provision of tenancy, inventory and credit check

Many landlords lose out on the opportunity to make extra money by charging tenants for services that they have to pay a letting agent for. It is reasonable to charge tenants anything from £50 up £150 to cover the cost of doing the inventory, tenant checks and providing the tenancy agreement.

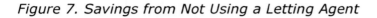

*Figure 7. Savings from Not Using a Letting Agent*

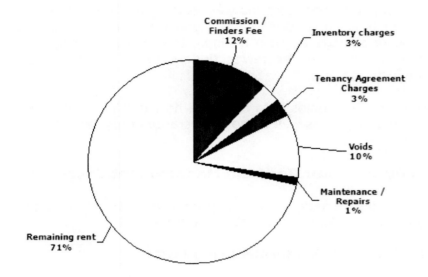

Applying this to the previously mentioned portfolio of 10 properties with 15 annual renewals, you could make an extra £1,500 which represents a 2.5% increase in the portfolio's rental income.

Assuming a portfolio of 10 properties each receiving £500 a month in rent and using the figures mentioned in the sections above, the potential savings from NOT using a letting agent are represented in the pie chart (Figure 7) above.

The total potential saving is 29% of the portfolio rental figure! This improves to over 31.5% when you add the gain from charging tenants a fee for carrying out the tenant check, inventory and providing the tenancy agreement. This means that by managing your portfolio yourself you could improve your cash position by almost a third which would certainly help alleviate the additional mortgage costs imposed by banks since the advent of the credit crunch.

How much you stand to save will obviously depend on your portfolio profile and the types of tenants, and repair and maintenance costs, as well as the turnover of tenants. If you have long-term tenants you would not necessarily achieve savings as high as indicated in the pie chart, as you would have far fewer finders fees, inventory and tenancy charges.

However, the point is to illustrate how quickly these costs can mount up, as well as how substantial they can be.

## Reducing Your Portfolio Management Costs

If you do manage your own properties the following tips will help you keep your costs to a minimum.

### 18 Essential Tips for Reducing Costs:

- Determine the best means of marketing each of your properties. Some properties will need to be advertised in your local newspaper, classifieds or on the internet. Try different methods and when you find one that works stick to it.

- Make sure you target the right tenants with accurate descriptions of the property and of the type of tenant you are looking for.

- If tenants call, develop a screening process. Ask them what they are looking for, do they have a partner and/or children, how much rent can they afford, what areas are they looking for, do they have employment references or references from a previous landlord, any pets, do they smoke, do they need parking, do they need a garden, do they have a deposit, can they pay one month rent upfront etc. It helps to get answers to all these questions upfront, otherwise you may waste time and money by finding out, for instance, they have two male Rottweilers the day before they move into your newly carpeted property!

- Explain that you charge a fee to cover tenant credit checks, inventory checks and the tenancy agreement, and that you require a guarantor (where necessary), along with proof of identification.

- If you don't have what they're looking for, don't say that – rather tell them you have properties becoming available soon and take their details. It's also possible to make a small commission by referring these tenants on to other landlords you may know.

- Try and get all your potential tenants to view on the same day, with 10 minute intervals between tenants. Not only does this save you time, but it also gives the impression the property is in demand and tenants will often decide on the spot.

- Always make sure you carry out a credit check on the tenant – there are various services available online at reasonable fees and this will certainly be worthwhile in ensuring quality tenants are placed.

- If the tenant is interested in taking your property, always ask for a non-refundable holding deposit. Not only does this ensure the tenant commits to the tenancy (there is nothing more frustrating than someone cancelling a tenancy a day before) but also compensates you for your time.

- When meeting the tenant to hand over keys, ensure you view documents proving the identity of the tenant and guarantor and get them to sign the inventory and tenancy agreements.

- A really useful tip is to identify tenants that may wish to swap between properties. I have on numerous occasions moved tenants between properties for a range of reasons: they may be expecting a baby so need an extra room, they may need to be closer to town or they may want to save some rent and move to a smaller place.

- Many landlords forget to take meter readings for gas and electricity, either when they purchase a new property or when the tenant moves in or out. This is vital to ensure that you are not charged any portion of usage that is not yours. Service providers (including water) will always try and bill you for services you have not used and the most common way they do this is by providing estimated readings.

  I once had a gas bill for £85 even though the property was empty and the boiler had been turned off. The property had been empty when I purchased it and one week later tenants moved in. Fortunately I had photographic evidence of the meter reading and was able to prove I was not liable for the bill. These costs end up being substantial over the course of a year, especially where large portfolios are involved. It is also useful to have all utility supplier contact details to give to all new tenants to speed up their connection where key and card meters are used.

- Ensure you inform the following organisations when new tenants move in and/or out: 1) the local council (for council tax) 2) water 3) gas and 4) electricity companies. It's worth taking note that some (not all) councils either charge zero or 50% council tax on properties that are currently empty, provided they are actively being marketed, so it is worth telling the council if you get even a week's void. Also, some councils will charge council tax on void properties if they are furnished or partly furnished.

- If a property is empty make sure you inform the water supplier as if it is on a service charge they may end up billing you during any void periods.

- If a property requires repairs or maintenance, ensure you get three different tradesmen to quote. Being lazy with obtaining quotes will normally cost you more than it should! Once you have found a reliable and reasonably priced tradesman you can keep using them.

- In instances where repairs may be very expensive to carry out, but the repair will not impact the living standards of the tenants, it may be more economical to offer the tenant a reduction in rent, rather than carrying out the repair. Although this is not the best long-term solution, it may be beneficial in the short term, especially where the repair may be better to carry out when the property is vacated.

- If a property is left in a poor state when vacated, it is sometimes easier to offer the new tenant (assuming they don't mind) a small cash incentive to accept the property as is, and do the cleaning themselves. This can, however, cause problems when referring to the inventory and the repayment of the deposit at the end of the tenancy.

- If you have carried out renovation work on a property, if there are any problems which arise, ensure you get the same tradesmen to carry out the repair. This way you won't pay for unnecessary costs by getting new tradesmen in.

- When a tradesman carries out a repair, always follow up the job by either contacting the tenant or viewing the work yourself. This will not only help clarify whether the tenant is happy with the repair but will show the tradesman that you expect a certain quality of work, and that they can't expect to pull a fast one on you!

I recently had a door lock fixed where the locksmith had charged me for 2-3 hours work. Before I paid, I checked with the tenant that the door was working and also asked how long the locksmith was there. The tenant mentioned he had only been there for 30 minutes! If I had not checked I would have paid for work not done – needless to say I not only got a reduction in my bill, but he offered some additional services for free for making the "invoicing mistake".

## Debt Collection

There are inevitably going to be instances where a tenant may have rental arrears and/or abandons a property, leaving it in such a state of disrepair that the deposit does not cover the rent arrears or the costs of repairing the property.

The risk can be greatly reduced if you carry out the necessary tenant credit checks, follow up on employment and previous landlord references, and obtain a guarantor.

If approaching the guarantor fails it is best to utilise the services of a debt collection agency. There are numerous firms offering similar services.

However, if the initial correspondence by the debt collectors, including the threat of litigation and ultimately bankruptcy does not prompt a response from the ex-tenant, it is costly and time consuming going the litigation route, and even then you are still not guaranteed to receive any money back.

I would recommend you discuss any specific debt related queries with a suitably qualified professional.

## Buildings & Contents Insurance

Most landlords, of course, have buildings insurance. It is also essential to have contents insurance to protect items that would be very expensive to replace such as kitchens and carpets.

The cost of buildings and contents insurance varies substantially and it is advisable to shop around and ask for different levels of cover with different excesses.

It is also advisable to use a company that will give you a portfolio policy which allows you to add properties that you buy and take off properties that you sell. This will cut your paperwork significantly.

One other tip is to always query the increase in premium when the policy is due for renewal. Insurers will usually put through a higher than expected increase, and in many cases landlords will typically overlook this extra cost.

My last policy increase was initially 9%. However, by calling the insurer and querying the reason for the increase I was able to get the same level of premium I paid the previous year. In some cases you may even get a reduction.

## Rent Insurance / Rent Guarantee

It is possible to obtain insurance to protect you in case a tenant falls behind on the rent, or for cases where tenants may not be able to pay the rent. Typically these insurance policies require the tenants pass credit checks undertaken by the insurer.

However, by carrying out your own due diligence on tenants and checking references, having a guarantor, having a deposit and doing your own tenant credit check, you should be confident in the quality of tenant you are placing, and if the tenant does fall behind on their rent you will be able to gain possession of the property by serving the relevant notices.

So in a way, by being prudent in qualifying a tenant before agreeing a tenancy, you don't need to incur the additional cost of insuring the rent.

However, landlords who are particularly risk averse may still want to take out this type of insurance. Included below is a summary of what cover is included and what is required in order to obtain a rent guarantee.

## Landlords Legal Expenses with Rent Guarantee

To claim on the landlords rent guarantee insurance you will need the following:

- A signed tenancy agreement

- Two forms of identification from the tenant, one of which must contain a clear photograph

- Proof of the tenant's employment

- A credit check

- A full tenant reference performed by an approved referencing company

In addition you will need to agree to the following:

- Each tenant will be referenced by a licenced tenant referencing service.

- If the tenant requires a guarantor or surety then the guarantor must be referenced by an approved tenant reference service.

- The tenant must sign an assured short-hold tenancy agreement before the property can be occupied.

- You must collect one month's rent in advance and a dilapidation deposit before the property can be occupied by the tenant.

- You must keep a record of all rent due and all rent paid.

Source: www.landlords-building-insurance.co.uk

## Corgi Certificates

For all rental properties which utilise gas it is a legal requirement to obtain a Corgi certificate once a year. Failure to do this carries penalties and other risks. That said, I am sometimes amazed at the exorbitant fees that some Corgi registered plumbers charge. I have heard of fees as high as £180, excluding VAT!

If you apply this to a portfolio of 10 properties that comes to £2,115, including VAT and represents 3.52% of the Portfolio Rental Figure. I would suggest getting quotes from various Corgi registered plumbers and when you find one that charges a reasonable fee (this can be anything from £45 to £80 depending on the area) ask what price they would charge for doing all your properties in that area.

Also ask them if they're VAT registered.

## Home Care Agreements

Having mentioned boilers, I often get asked about the viability of utilising 'home care agreements' which cover the breakdown of boilers, and can also include all plumbing, pipes, electrics etc. While these may be ideal for landlords who want minimum hassle from repairs required, there are drawbacks.

Before being accepted on a policy, an engineer typically inspects the property you want insured. In cases where they have grounds to condemn a boiler (in which case you are legally not allowed to continue using it) you have to resort to either expensive repairs which can take weeks to complete or, in some cases, replace the boiler.

There is an argument that the engineers are more inclined to condemn boilers that can reasonably be repaired as they can make more commission from a replacement than a repair (I know several landlords who have had this experience).

I also know landlords who, upon having their boilers condemned, have brought in their own boiler engineers who have managed to repair the boiler or, where a replacement was needed, do this at sometimes half the cost.

Of course not everyone will have this problem. The bottom line is that by deciding to take up a home care agreement you may be exposing yourself to large repair or replacement costs, as well as void periods if the property remains empty while the work is carried out.

## Energy Performance Certificates (EPC)

Under new EU legislation which comes into force from October 1st 2008, when buildings are to be sold or rented out, the landlord is responsible for ensuring a valid Energy Performance Certificate is made available to all prospective purchasers and tenants.

Each property's certificate is valid for 10 years and the prices range from £70 to £100, depending on the location of your properties.

However, if modernisation work is carried out it may be advantageous to have the property re-assessed to reflect the improvements.

If you have a sizeable portfolio it may be worthwhile scheduling the works with either one company, or a group of affiliated companies.

# CHAPTER 9

# Should I Sell My Properties?

Most landlords are long-term investors and plan to ride out the credit crunch and wait for prices to recover. However, certain groups of investors may be considering selling:

- Those close to retirement, who cannot wait many years for prices to recover.

- Investors with very unhealthy portfolios. Those making big rental losses and watching the value of their properties fall each month have less incentive to wait for the recovery. This group may wish to sell some properties to release cash to reduce the mortgages on others.

- Aggressive investors who believe prices will fall a lot further and wish to snap up bargains later on.

In theory, you could save yourself a fortune by selling before prices drop any further. For example, if you have a property currently worth £250,000 and prices drop a further 20%, your potential loss is £50,000. If you have a portfolio of 10 properties worth £125,000 each, your potential loss is £250,000.

The problem with this strategy is costs. Selling property is expensive, as is buying property. If you sell some or all of your portfolio now and reinvest in a couple of year's time, your savings may not outweigh the selling and buying costs.

And remember, you won't be selling at the top of the market. The price you can achieve today may be a lot lower than the price you could have achieved 12 months ago.

The important point to remember is that house price crashes do bottom out and eventually prices will start increasing again! There have been three other property crashes in the last 40 years (1975, 1980 and 1990) and each time prices did return to their previous levels.

What is worrying, however, is that each time there has been a house price crash, it has taken longer and longer for prices to recover (see Figure 2). The 1990s crash took a very long time to unravel. Real house prices peaked in 1989 and only returned to those levels at the end of 2001. In other words, it took 12 years before property investors recouped all their losses.

If you find yourself in a position where the bulk of your wealth is tied up in your home or buy-to-let portfolio, then you should take an urgent look at your medium and long-term goals and decide whether you stand to gain or lose by selling now.

Another important point to remember is:

**You only actually lose money when you sell your property!**

If you could have sold your house last year for £300,000 and this year you can only sell it for £270,000, you have not actually lost £30,000. You'll only lose this wealth if you sell the property now.

Others would argue that if you wait any longer, you'll lose even more money. For example, if you sell the same house in a year's time you may only get £240,000.

This argument is valid but only if you are likely to have to sell. What I can say with certainty is that house prices will recover. What I cannot predict is how far prices will go down and how long it will take for them to bounce back.

## Inflation Danger

The longer property prices take to recover the more you have to worry about inflation. UK inflation is currently running at around 4% and rising.

For example, looking at the 1990s property downturn, *nominal* house prices started falling at the end of 1989 and had fully recovered by the beginning of 1998. *Real* house prices (adjusted for inflation) took until the beginning of 2002 to recover – four years later!

What this means is that the average property owner didn't make a single penny out of property between 1989 and 2002.

If you're an investor it's essential to only look at the real value of your investments. After all, £100,000 in five years time is worth a lot less than £100,000 today.

It's impossible to predict what will happen to real property prices this time around but what you should always remember is that, unless your properties are growing at least as fast as inflation, you are in fact losing money each year!

## Costs

If you plan to sell some properties and reinvest later on, you have to weigh up the costs. These can be divided into exit costs and entrance costs.

Exit costs are all your selling costs and include:

- **Estate agent fees** – typically up to 2% of the value of the property

- **Legal fees** – solicitors typically charge up to £1,000

Entrance costs are all the fees and charges you will rack up when you reinvest and include:

- **Legal fees** – up to £1,000 but possibly more in a few years time.

- **Survey fees** – currently up to £450, possibly more in a few years time.

- **Stamp duty** – Currently 1% on properties bought for between £125,000 and £249,999, 3% stamp duty from £250,000.

- **Mortgage fees** – Mortgage fees have increased significantly over the last 12 months, with some lenders charging 2.5% of the property's purchase price.

### Example

*Dave owns two properties worth £500,000, with equity of £250,000. If he sells them and then reinvests a few years later, his costs might look something like this:*

*Exit Fees:*
*Estate agents fees (2% per property)*        *£10,000*
*Legal fees (£1,000 per property)*        *£2,000*

*Entrance Fees (a few years later):*

| | |
|---|---|
| *Legal fees* | *£2,400* |
| *Survey fees* | *£600* |
| *Stamp duty* | *£5,000* |
| *Mortgage fees* | *£5,000* |

**Total Exit and Entrance Costs**      *£25,000*

Capital gains tax would also need to be considered and added on to this total cost. Assuming a capital gains tax bill of £30,000, Dave's total buying and selling costs come to £55,000.


## The Costs Most of Us Forget

Dave's costs could get a lot uglier, however. He also has to watch out for:

*Mortgage Redemption Charges*

When you sell your property you may have to pay an early redemption charge on your mortgage. These penalties usually range from around 1% to 5% of the mortgage. If Dave finds himself in this predicament he could have to stump up another £2,500 to £12,500 to his lender.

*Mortgage Interest*

From the day Dave decides to put the property on the market until the day his solicitor receives payment from the buyer he will have to pay mortgage interest. With properties taking longer and longer to sell this could easily come to another £8,000.

*Property Contents*

Another cost most people forget are the property's contents. If you sell your property you'll probably also have to sell all the furniture, beds and appliances. You'll probably only get a pittance for them but will pay a lot more when you eventually buy another property and furnish it. The cost to Dave? Easily another £2,000.

The question Dave has to ask himself is whether he will save *more* money by selling before house prices fall even further.

The answer would probably have been yes at the peak of the property market. However, this question is much more difficult to answer if you're trying to offload property when the market is weak, buyers are scarce and prices are falling.

For many investors the exit and entrance costs may be too high to absorb – a significant percentage of your property wealth will be decimated by costs and tax if you sell now and reinvest later on.

CHAPTER 10

# Strategies to Protect Your Home & Personal Finances

**Sell or Rent?**

Because the property market is so weak at present, more and more people are renting out their homes instead of selling them, especially those who have to relocate for work or other reasons.

This strategy has benefits and drawbacks.

The benefit is you could end up saving a lot of money if you can ride out the credit crunch and wait for house prices to recover. In the meantime you can rent out the property and use the income to pay your own rent somewhere else.

*(There are some legal issues to consider, such as checking with your mortgage and insurance providers that it's OK to rent out the property.)*

For many people this scenario may allow them the flexibility of keeping their primary residence, while possibly saving money by renting a cheaper property.

However, whether this strategy is ultimately worth pursuing depends on your long-term goals and it's also important to realize the risks. If you hold onto the property but end up having to sell it in a couple of years time, when prices have fallen by perhaps another 20%, then you'd have been better off taking your medicine now.

Homeowners should not necessarily worry about falling house prices. If your home was worth £400,000 last year but is only worth £350,000 today, you won't lose any money if the property you move to is also £50,000 cheaper than it was 12 months ago.

Those homeowners who stand to lose most from the credit crunch include those who are:

- **Downsizing**. A lot of people plan to use the wealth in their homes as an additional form of pension saving. For example, if you sell your home worth £400,000 and go and live in a property costing £250,000, you can release a tax-free lump sum of £150,000. Most people's property pension savings have fallen dramatically in the last 12 months.

- **Relocating**. If you have to move from an area where the property market is weak to an area where the market is stronger you will also lose out because you may not be able to buy your new home at an equivalent discount.

One thing every homeowner should watch out for in a falling market is legally committing to buy a new property before the old home is sold. If you struggle to find a buyer and have to mark down the price substantially you could end up in a serious predicament, especially if you have used bridging finance to buy the new property.

## Improving Your Existing Home

Instead of selling, many homeowners are staying put and adding improvements to their existing homes.

It can work out far cheaper to build an extension than upgrade to a bigger property because you won't incur any selling and buying costs (estate agent fees, solicitors fees, stamp duty etc).

If you make the right choices you could add significant value to the property and in many cases it will be relatively easy to obtain the necessary finance.

What remains to be seen is whether building costs will fall as the downturn in the property market deepens. In theory, as home builders lay off workers, there will be more people competing for less work, so it should be possible to obtain more competitive quotes.

## Interest Rate Insurance

There's a new type of insurance being offered called Interest Rate Insurance (IRI). Marketguard (marketguard.com) recently launched this product for people who want to protect against dramatic increases in interest rates.

With inflation rising rapidly there is a danger the Bank of England will have to raise interest rates to rein it in, even though the economy is very weak.

Marketguard offers the insurance for both residential and buy-to-let mortgages, so this product could be useful for homeowners, as well as landlords. It is worth noting that the buy-to-let insurance is substantially cheaper than the residential IRI. The insurance is available for variable and tracker mortgages and fixed-rate mortgages which have no more than three months left to run.

The product does not protect you if your interest rate increases simply because you have moved from a fixed-rate deal onto your lender's standard variable rate.

You will also not be covered for increases in interest rates up to the policy's 'excess'. You choose the level of excess you want when you take out the insurance. For example, you can choose to be protected only after interest rates go up by, say, 1%. The higher the excess the lower the monthly premium.

A typical premium for a £100,000 mortgage with a 1% excess could be around £25 per month; for a 2% excess the premium would be about £12.50 per month. To get more accurate costs it is best to contact Marketguard directly.

In some cases the policy costs may not warrant the potential savings available and many might argue that interest rates will not go up drastically while the economy is so weak.

However, with inflation rising rapidly and banks desperate to repair their balance sheets, it's impossible to predict what will happen to rates in the months ahead.

It is ultimately up to landlords and homeowners to decide what level of interest rate volatility they can afford.

This is a complex product and I would recommend that you speak to a financial advisor before taking the plunge.

## Paying Off Your Debt

In times of economic uncertainty one of the best things you can do with any spare cash is reduce your debts.

The UK has never been in so much debt.

Consider the following statistics from Credit Action:

- Average consumer borrowing via credit cards, motor and retail finance deals, overdrafts and unsecured personal loans has on average risen to £4,900 per adult.

- Average household debt is £9,341 (excluding mortgages).

- This figure rises to £21,725 if the average is based on the number of households who actually have some form of unsecured loan.

- UK debt grows by £1 million every 5 minutes.

If you want to reduce your debt consider the following pointers.

- Pay off the loans with the highest interest rates first. In general this would mean paying off credit cards before you pay off your mortgages (unless you can make a credit card balance transfer and postpone interest for several months).

- Pay off non-tax deductible loans first. Credit card interest and home mortgage interest is generally NOT tax deductible. Interest on buy-to-let mortgages and business loans is generally tax deductible. Interest that is not tax deductible is more 'expensive' so you should generally pay if off first.

- However, you should consider reducing your buy-to-let mortgages if this means you can get a better deal when you remortgage. Most buy-to-let lenders insist that you have at least 25% equity in the property. I've also seen products offering competitive interest rates but only for those with at least 50% equity.

- Watch out for mortgage redemption penalties. Many lenders will penalize you heavily if you pay off any of the mortgage before your fixed-rate deal expires.

Be wary of paying off debt if that could leave you strapped for cash. Make sure you can still access the funds. Some mortgages allow you to make withdrawals, others do not.

In some instances it may be more prudent to build a cash reserve to protect against increased mortgage payments or unexpected cash flow problems, such as the loss of your primary source of income.

For example, if you have £20,000 in a high interest savings account and a £200,000 mortgage, using the money to reduce your mortgage will reduce your monthly payments by about £100, which will probably not make a huge difference to your financial situation.

However, if the money remains at your disposal in a savings account, it could be used to pay the entire mortgage for around 20 months. This could make a huge difference if you lose your primary source of income.

Cash reserves can also be used to exploit opportunities later on.


## Portfolio Mortgages

Some lenders will take a blanket approach to your portfolio and allow you to balance properties that have high LTVs but very good rental coverage with properties that may have low LTVs but very poor rental coverage.

This may enable you to release equity from properties that have low LTVs.

Another advantage of using a portfolio mortgage is that there is far less admin and paperwork involved and in some cases you may have your own account manager.

If you need to remortgage this can often be done over the phone and there is sometimes no need for lengthy forms to be filled in. Also, access to draw down facilities can be arranged easily and quickly and can certainly help you when you need access to additional cash resources.

There are however conditions that may limit your use of portfolio mortgages, with many lenders having a cap on the number of properties or the total value of mortgages that one client can hold. In these instances, and depending on the size of your portfolio, you may have to spread your portfolio over a number of portfolio mortgage providers.

It can be tricky deciding which properties should be held with which lender. You don't want to be in a position where all your equity is held by one portfolio mortgage company.

It is best to speak to a suitably qualified professional who can advise you what products are available and what route to take.

# CHAPTER 11

# Maximizing Your Portfolio Cashflow

A very useful exercise is to look at an overall summary of your portfolio's cash flow position, to see which properties are making you the most money, and which properties are losing you the most money.

One simple way of doing this is to construct what I call a Portfolio Summary Sheet, as illustrated in Figure 8 below.

Doing this will help you identify possible areas of improvement, for example those properties which require an increase in rental or those requiring the highest level of repairs. It may be better to sell those properties that are losing you the most money and do not offer scope for rental increases.

Looking at Figure 8 you can quickly see which properties have the lowest rental cover and which properties have the highest loan to value. You may, of course, wish to hang on to these properties if, for example, they are new or offer scope for above average capital growth, or if the mortgage redemption penalties would be substantial.

*Figure 8. Portfolio Summary Sheet*

| No | Property Address | Mortgage Outstanding | Current Market Value of Property | Net Equity | Loan to Value | Rental Income | Monthly Mortgage Payment | Rental Coverage |
|---|---|---|---|---|---|---|---|---|
| 1 | 16 Fairy Way | £153,313 | £175,000 | £21,687 | 88% | £695 | £689 | 101% |
| 2 | 49 Ranfield Lane | £156,860 | £185,000 | £28,140 | 85% | £780 | £685 | 114% |
| 3 | 57 Rageby Road | £112,500 | £135,000 | £22,500 | 83% | £595 | £567 | 105% |
| 4 | 26a Essington Street | £56,250 | £72,000 | £15,750 | 78% | £360 | £283 | 127% |
| 5 | 26 Essington Street | £56,250 | £72,000 | £15,750 | 78% | £350 | £283 | 124% |
| 6 | 81 Westrel Lane | £77,839 | £95,000 | £17,161 | 82% | £495 | £402 | 123% |
| 7 | 23 Course Way | £138,575 | £169,000 | £30,425 | 82% | £650 | £636 | 102% |
| 8 | 25 Lampton Court | £103,122 | £125,000 | £21,878 | 82% | £525 | £467 | 112% |
| 9 | 38 Steinheim Walk | £112,192 | £129,000 | £16,808 | 87% | £575 | £550 | 105% |
| 10 | 53 Scarborough Street | £72,000 | £85,000 | £13,000 | 85% | £400 | £379 | 105% |
| 11 | 18 Glenn Close | £102,000 | £125,000 | £23,000 | 82% | £525 | £469 | 112% |
| 12 | 27 Ralcote Drive | £220,958 | £265,000 | £44,042 | 83% | £1,350 | £1,080 | 125% |
| 13 | 59 Scarborough Street | £72,000 | £85,000 | £13,000 | 85% | £400 | £336 | 119% |
| 14 | 87 Scarborough Street | £68,000 | £85,000 | £17,000 | 80% | £400 | £344 | 116% |
| 15 | 114 Scarborough Street | £72,000 | £85,000 | £13,000 | 85% | £400 | £344 | 116% |
| 16 | 74 Southfields | £102,000 | £120,000 | £18,000 | 85% | £525 | £415 | 127% |
| 17 | 70 Eastline | £102,000 | £120,000 | £18,000 | 85% | £525 | £499 | 105% |
| 18 | 38 Scatter Walk | £103,700 | £120,000 | £16,300 | 86% | £525 | £428 | 123% |
| 19 | 18 Woulstow Close | £60,987 | £78,000 | £17,013 | 78% | £375 | £289 | 130% |
| 20 | 18A Woulstow Close | £60,987 | £78,000 | £17,013 | 78% | £350 | £289 | 121% |
| | TOTAL | £2,003,532 | £2,403,000 | £399,468 | 83% | £10,800 | £9,434 | 114% |

To download a free useable Portfolio Summary Sheet please visit: www.taxcafe.co.uk/creditcrunchlinks.html

The important point is that a snapshot of your portfolio's health will help you target areas for improvement.

Looking at Figure 8, it would appear that with an overall rental coverage of 114% this portfolio is in pretty good shape. No money is being lost on any of the properties because the rents are higher than the mortgage costs. The landlord is making £1,366 per month (£10,800 rent less £9,434 in mortgages), which comes to £16,392 per year!

Furthermore the portfolio has an overall loan to value ratio of 83.3% which equates to total equity of £399,468.

Now let me ask you two questions:

- Do you feel the portfolio shown in Figure 8 is healthy?

- In which quadrant of the Landlord Health Diagram (Figure 1) would you put this landlord?

You would naturally say that as the landlord is making a rental profit of £1,366 a month and has substantial equity this portfolio is relatively healthy and the landlord could be described as lying somewhere between quadrants 1 (Property Tycoon) and 2 (Busy Investor), which is not a bad place to be.

I would agree with this **but...**

As any landlord knows there are always other costs to worry about, including repairs, maintenance, void periods, advertising etc.

I generally work these out at an average of 7% of the gross rent. In this example, the gross rent is £10,800 per month so these extra costs would come to £756 per month.

The monthly rental profit therefore falls from £1,366 to £610. Although the investor is still making a profit, he is creeping closer to the middle of the Landlord Health Diagram (Figure 1).

## Interest Rate Danger

This is one of the most important sections of this book! I have previously mentioned that: *Landlords have to know their cash flow position over the next 12 – 18 months!*

You may have glanced over this and stored it away in a section of your brain titled: Interesting but meaningless stuff! Let me now show you why this exercise is **ABSOLUTELY IMPERATIVE!** Figure 9 below shows the projected cash flow for our landlord from April 2008 until May 2009.

The landlord starts off with a decent bank balance of £5,000 and after adding all rental income and deducting mortgage interest plus 7% for all other costs (voids, repairs etc), ends up with £5,610 in his bank account at the end of April 2008.

The cells highlighted in grey show sudden decreases in profits which occur when our landlord's fixed-rate mortgage deals come to an end.

The initial interest rates that our landlord was paying in April 2008 are shown at the far right of the table. For example, 16 Fairy Way is currently on a fixed interest rate of 5.39%.

Now taking into account lenders currently strict remortgage criteria, it is likely our landlord will at best secure a 7% interest rate.

*Figure 9. Projected Cash Flow Forecast for Portfolio*

| No | Property Address | Apr-08 | May-08 | Jun-08 | Jul-08 | Aug-08 | Sep-08 | Oct-08 | Nov-08 | Dec-08 | Jan-09 | Mar-09 | Apr-09 | May-09 | Initial Interest Rate |
|---|---|---|---|---|---|---|---|---|---|---|---|---|---|---|---|
| 1 | 16 Fairy Way | -£42 | -£248 | -£248 | -£248 | -£248 | -£248 | -£248 | -£248 | -£248 | -£248 | -£248 | -£248 | -£248 | 5.39% |
| 2 | 49 Ranfield Lane | £40 | £40 | -£190 | -£190 | -£190 | -£190 | -£190 | -£190 | -£190 | -£190 | -£190 | -£190 | -£190 | 5.24% |
| 3 | 57 Rageby Road | -£14 | -£103 | -£103 | -£103 | -£103 | -£103 | -£103 | -£103 | -£103 | -£103 | -£103 | -£103 | -£103 | 6.05% |
| 4 | 26a Essington Street | £52 | £52 | £7 | £7 | £7 | £7 | £7 | £7 | £7 | £7 | £7 | £7 | £7 | 6.04% |
| 5 | 26 Essington Street | £42 | £42 | £42 | -£3 | -£3 | -£3 | -£3 | -£3 | -£3 | -£3 | -£3 | -£3 | -£3 | 6.04% |
| 6 | 81 Westrel Lane | £59 | £59 | £6 | £6 | £6 | £6 | £6 | £6 | £6 | £6 | £6 | £6 | £6 | 6.19% |
| 7 | 23 Course Way | -£31 | -£204 | -£204 | -£204 | -£204 | -£204 | -£204 | -£204 | -£204 | -£204 | -£204 | -£204 | -£204 | 5.50% |
| 8 | 25 Lampton Court | £21 | £21 | £21 | -£113 | -£113 | -£113 | -£113 | -£113 | -£113 | -£113 | -£113 | -£113 | -£113 | 5.44% |
| 9 | 38 Steinheim Walk | -£15 | -£120 | -£120 | -£120 | -£120 | -£120 | -£120 | -£120 | -£120 | -£120 | -£120 | -£120 | -£120 | 5.88% |
| 10 | 53 Scarborough Street | -£7 | -£7 | -£7 | -£48 | -£48 | -£48 | -£48 | -£48 | -£48 | -£48 | -£48 | -£48 | -£48 | 6.32% |
| 11 | 18 Glenn Close | £19 | £19 | £19 | £19 | -£107 | -£107 | -£107 | -£107 | -£107 | -£107 | -£107 | -£107 | -£107 | 5.52% |
| 12 | 27 Ralcote Drive | £176 | £176 | £176 | £176 | -£33 | -£33 | -£33 | -£33 | -£33 | -£33 | -£33 | -£33 | -£33 | 5.86% |
| 13 | 59 Scarborough Street | £36 | £36 | -£48 | -£48 | -£48 | -£48 | -£48 | -£48 | -£48 | -£48 | -£48 | -£48 | -£48 | 5.60% |
| 14 | 87 Scarborough Street | £28 | -£25 | -£25 | -£25 | -£25 | -£25 | -£25 | -£25 | -£25 | -£25 | -£25 | -£25 | -£25 | 6.06% |
| 15 | 114 Scarborough Street | £28 | £28 | -£48 | -£48 | -£48 | -£48 | -£48 | -£48 | -£48 | -£48 | -£48 | -£48 | -£48 | 5.73% |
| 16 | 74 Southfields | £74 | £74 | £74 | -£107 | -£107 | -£107 | -£107 | -£107 | -£107 | -£107 | -£107 | -£107 | -£107 | 4.88% |
| 17 | 70 Eastline | -£10 | -£10 | -£107 | -£107 | -£107 | -£107 | -£107 | -£107 | -£107 | -£107 | -£107 | -£107 | -£107 | 5.87% |
| 18 | 38 Scatter Walk | £60 | £60 | -£117 | -£117 | -£117 | -£117 | -£117 | -£117 | -£117 | -£117 | -£117 | -£117 | -£117 | 4.96% |
| 19 | 18 Woulstow Close | £60 | £60 | £60 | -£7 | -£7 | -£7 | -£7 | -£7 | -£7 | -£7 | -£7 | -£7 | -£7 | 5.69% |
| 20 | 18A Woulstow Close | £37 | -£30 | -£30 | -£30 | -£30 | -£30 | -£30 | -£30 | -£30 | -£30 | -£30 | -£30 | -£30 | 5.69% |
| | TOTAL | £610 | -£82 | -£842 | -£1,309 | -£1,643 | -£1,643 | -£1,643 | -£1,643 | -£1,643 | -£1,643 | -£1,643 | -£1,643 | -£1,643 | |
| | BANK BALANCE | £5,610 | £5,529 | £4,687 | £3,378 | £1,735 | £92 | -£1,552 | -£3,195 | -£4,838 | -£6,481 | -£8,125 | -£9,768 | -£11,411 | |

To download a useable Projected Cash Flow Forecast sheet please visit:
www.taxcafe.co.uk/creditcrunchlinks.html

What should stick out like a sore thumb is that by the end of May 2009, our landlord's bank balance has become overdrawn to the tune of **£11,411**! From a relatively healthy position of having £5,610 in the bank as of April 2008, our landlord has ended up losing a total of **£17,021** in less than a year.

---

**This is the biggest threat to landlords at the moment!**

Many landlords will not fully understand the implications of the mortgage drought, higher mortgage interest rates, falling property prices and lower LTVs being offered by lenders.

Together these can turn a relatively healthy portfolio which was making a decent rental profit into a critically unhealthy portfolio and turn a borderline Property Tycoon into a Nervous Novice!

---

# CHAPTER 12

# How to Make Money Out of the Credit Crunch

Even with the current economic and financial turmoil there are still opportunities to make money in property!

However, the mantra that anyone can make money in property has never been more wrong. It may be more accurate to say that it has never been easier to lose money!

The traditional model of simply buying property and hoping the price will go up is pretty much dead.

Subsidizing properties when the mortgage and maintenance costs were higher than the rent was fine when property prices were increasing. Following the same model today will end up in bankruptcy.

With potentially 12 years to wait until property prices return to their previous highs, the professional landlord will now be looking more at generating cash by adding value to properties and achieving higher yields.

Some of the ways professional landlords are now making money is by moving into other disciplines and using different investing methods. These are detailed below:

## Sell Equity in Your Existing Portfolio

This is something that can work in rare situations. It typically involves selling a share of equity in a property for a cash lump sum.

The equity buyer typically has to be someone with whom the investor has an established relationship because there's an element of trust involved – the property owner undertakes to give the equity buyer a share in the property and agrees to pay this at some time in the future.

You would need to consult a solicitor to set up such an agreement and it may not be possible if your mortgage lender does not agree.

Assuming the mortgage company agrees to the second charge and assuming a solicitor can work out an agreement both parties are happy with, this can be an effective means of raising funds when an investor with equity cannot extract cash through the traditional mortgage route.

## Creating Goldmines!

I know many landlords who are sitting on goldmines but do not know it! This is because they do not consider the possibilities of re-defining a property. Let me explain.

There are countless properties that have been converted into flats but are still on one freehold title.

Examples may include a two storey terraced house that was converted into two one-bedroom flats, or a three storey Victorian house that was converted into three two-bedroom flats.

The commercial value of these types of properties can be greatly improved if the properties are put onto separate leases and as such can be either individually remortgaged or sold.

In my experience, this strategy can add as much as 70% to the value of the property.

To illustrate, I purchased a terraced house for £75,000 which was on one freehold title but had been converted into two one-bedroom self contained flats. Similar two bed terraced houses sold for £70,000 on the same street, so I paid a slight premium.

However, once I had refurbished the flats at a cost of £7,000 and created two separate leases at a cost of £1,500 in solicitor's fees, I was able to remortgage the flats with a value of £65,000 each.

Hence, I was able to turn a £75,000 asset into an asset now worth £130,000, for just £8,500! Not only has the commercial value improved but there is additional potential to create value by selling on the freehold.

Depending on how you structure the leases i.e. the amount you charge for ground rent, freeholds can sell for significant sums.

Looking at recent auction sales, a freehold for a block of four two-bed leasehold flats, with a ground rent of £500 per annum per flat (i.e. £2,000 total annual ground rent) sold for £30,000.

This is one of the easiest ways of making money from property, however, there are various considerations such as:

- The level of ground rent, if set too high, may hamper the marketability of the property. Charging £1,000 per annum ground rent on a one-bed flat will likely lead to you being unable to find a buyer! Set the ground rent at a reasonable level.

- The initial purchase of the property can provide problems if the relevant planning consent and building regulations approval were not obtained. Ensure you use a suitably qualified professional to look at the property's legal documents (including land charges and title deeds) before purchasing.

  You don't want to be stuck with an illegal property. I know a landlord who purchased a three storey detached property at auction that had been converted into five one-bedroom flats. Unfortunately, he did not realise the property had never had planning permission to be converted. The council forced him to convert it back to a single residential dwelling with no recourse to appeal.

- There are numerous legal issues that your solicitor may need to address. Use one who has actually created leases before. I have come across many properties that have such poor leases they cannot be sold unless the leases are rectified (eg, buildings insurance not included as an obligation for the landlord, hence if the property burns down, the leaseholder cannot recoup any money). Also, the inclusion of service charge provisions enabling landlords to reclaim the cost of repairs to the fabric of the building from leaseholders is often overlooked.

## Purchasing New Properties:
## An Effective Way to Restructure a Portfolio

An astute landlord will focus on purchasing properties at below market value, or properties whose values can be greatly increased through refurbishment.

He will also focus on buying properties whose overall rent position can be improved.

The last thing you want is a property that does not earn enough rent or requires numerous costly repairs, or is in an area of weak tenant demand.

Properties like this will suck cash out of your pockets. Remember the only reason for investing should be to put money into your pocket!

Add this to the existing economic climate and the relatively high level of mortgage interest rates, along with the ever increasing rental cover and lower LTVs required by lenders, it is becoming increasingly more difficult for even seasoned landlords to find good deals.

There are however new opportunities that arise due to the uncertainty in the housing market. Let me illustrate:

I recently purchased two properties from another landlord who needed to free up cash for a new project he was undertaking.

From previous experience the landlord knew that I could complete quickly and would not have problems securing finance with different lenders.

The properties required some minor cosmetic refurbishment, including carpet cleaning, general cleaning and painting throughout.

The previous landlord evicted the tenants from both properties some months earlier and so was not receiving any rental income either. However, I knew the local area and was confident I could get a rent 20% higher than he was originally asking.

So I made an offer that was 25% below the confirmed valuation of the property and, after completing one month later, had all the necessary repair work carried out within one week and had tenants move in before the painting was finished.

I ended up getting two properties with 25% equity and rental coverage of 140% on both! I not only managed to gain by purchasing at a price significantly below the market value, but perhaps more importantly added a strong additional stream of rent to my existing rental stream.

Most landlords do not pay enough attention to this but one of the most effective ways of improving your overall rent is by ensuring you get the best possible price when purchasing. This involves good negotiating when first viewing prospective properties.

Not only does a reduction in price ensure you pay less on your mortgage, it also gives you more scope to get better mortgage deals as your loan to value ratio will be smaller which means lenders will give you better rates. Furthermore, the gap between the rent you earn and the mortgage you pay will be wider, which means more profit.

## Below Market Value (BMV) Method

This method generally involves buying property from distressed sellers (also known as 'motivated' sellers!).

It's a market that will probably grow and grow as more and more people struggle with higher mortgage interest rates and unemployment rises.

In the last housing crash in the 1990s unemployment peaked at 10%. If the same happens during the current economic downturn, an estimated 1.2 million more people will find themselves without a job.

It is these people who will be desperate to extract equity from their properties to help cover day to day living expenses. In the existing climate, there are an estimated 12 sellers for every buyer and many homeowners who find themselves out of work will be extremely motivated to sell at terms preferable to willing property investors.

Traditionally this type of below market value (BMV) purchasing involved establishing the current market value of the property through looking at comparable sales and then negotiating a discount – the more desperate the seller, the higher the discount.

Investors often find these properties by doing their own advertising: leaflet drops, adverts in local newspapers and shop windows. Some also purchase leads from property companies that specialize in this area.

Looking at various online forums, it seems that buyers of below market value properties are expecting much larger discounts now to protect against falling property prices.

Last year a 15% discount was a good deal, now it's 25%!

A problem facing many BMV investors has been the drying up of finance available to carry out this type of deal, most notably the withdrawal of 'day one' remortgage products. These allowed you to buy property with no money down.

What investors would do is use bridging finance for a day and then immediately remortgage the property. To remortgage a property you need equity but you don't need a deposit so investors were able to get 100% of the money required to buy the property and sometimes some extra spending cash too!

This type of loan has effectively become extinct with no lenders allowing you to remortgage within six months of buying a property. There are ways of getting round this, however, the legality of these techniques is often questionable and I would not want to make any suggestions on these strategies.

This is not the end of below market value investing, however, and many investors are prepared to wait to remortgage. I have even heard of investors using credit cards to pay the initial deposit!

There are two main risks to this strategy:

- Lenders may further tighten their criteria and only allow you to remortgage after 12 months.

- Falling house prices may eat up your equity in the property and make it difficult to remortgage.

Another factor to consider is that many of the people who sell their houses using this below market value method end up renting their house from the buyer. This is termed 'sale and rent back' and the press has picked up on people being made homeless once the initial tenancy expires.

As a result more and more people are calling for regulation of this industry. If this happens it is hard to say what the exact outcome will be but it is highly likely that any changes will **not** be in favour of investors buying these properties.

In some case investors are exploiting people, however it is difficult to say if this is common practice. Perhaps the Government will force the buyers to give the tenants lifetime tenancies with capped rental increases and first right of refusal should the landlord wish to sell the property.

Any regulation would obviously make these types of investments less attractive for landlords. However, until the issue comes to a head, it is likely there will still be lots of people looking at purchasing these properties.

## Should You Buy Property Now?

Why would anyone would want to buy a property in an environment of falling house prices.

People hoping to make a quick profit by buying cheap and selling on won't be able to make any money in the current climate as there are very few buyers around, shopping in a sea of properties for sale.

However, people who are wanting to invest funds with a view to getting a return on their investment through decent rental income growth and who are willing to hold onto a property for a relatively long time, say at least 12 years, will still be looking at buying property... providing the price is right.

### Example

*Sandra finds someone willing to sell their property at a 30% discount because they have just lost their job.*

*The current market value is £143,000 and Sandra secures a buying price of £100,000 (30% below the current market price).*

*The seller wants to stay on in the property as a tenant and agrees to pay a monthly rent of £833 which means the property has a rental yield of 10% (Sandra is a pretty shrewd negotiator).*

Let's say the seller is happy because he will end up with a significant cash windfall from selling because he only had a mortgage of £50,000.

Assuming Sandra gets a buy-to-let mortgage of 75% of the purchase price (£75,000) and secures a mortgage with an interest rate of 7%, her monthly mortgage will be £438. So immediately Sandra will be making a rental profit of £395 per month, which comes to £4,740 per year.

Given that she has had to invest £25,000 as a deposit, this works out to a 19% return. You might think this is a pretty good return, however there is one more step in Sandra's master plan.

After she has owned the property for six months she applies for a remortgage based on the current market value of £143,000 and gets a remortgage at 75% LTV – a total of £107,250. (This is assuming that there is no reduction in house prices.)

Hence, Sandra has managed to not only get back her initial £25,000 deposit but has also secured an additional £7,250.

Sandra's new monthly mortgage repayment is £626, so even after getting her initial investment back, and some extra cash in hand, she is still making a rental profit of £207 per month, or £2,484 profit per year!

For those investors willing to take the risk of putting down a hefty 25% deposit for a 6 month period, and perhaps 12 month period if banks further tighten their lending criteria, this may seem like an attractive deal.

The number of homeowners willing to sell their properties at a deep discount may be set to increase as more and more feel the effects of higher mortgage interest rates, higher inflation and, in the worst case scenario, unemployment.

Some argue that buying property this way amounts to exploitation of desperate people. However, my argument is that without investors willing to buy their homes, this group of individuals could actually end up worse off because their homes will be repossessed if they can't keep up with the mortgage payments.

## Properties Requiring Major Refurbishment

As I mentioned in the introduction to this book, I have carried out a lot of projects involving major refurbishment of properties.

These are properties with ceilings that have caved in because roof tiles are broken, windows that have been broken by evicted tenants, smashed in doors... the list goes on.

When many amateur investors think about this type of property they have visions of TV programmes showing DIY enthusiasts spending every last penny of their savings refurbishing the property, just to end up making £10 profit!

I do have two criteria that I insist on, however, and these are:

- The property must be structurally sound

- The property must not be located in a vandalism hotspot

More often than not structural issues are a precursor to even more problems. I tend to look at the symmetry of rooms – do the walls meet at right angles, are door frames perpendicular, windows square, floors level, are there any major cracks showing, is the roof sound (in some cases leaks can be caused by a cracked roof tile or blocked gutter which is easy enough to repair)?

I also always look at the property's exterior, including the roof. I am certainly not an expert in surveying, however, so I will never buy a property unless my builder and a surveyor first confirm they are happy with it.

As for vandalism, I have heard horror stories of landlords who have been 95% of the way through a project only to come back on the last day to find their property has been completely trashed.

I don't want to have to worry about a property while it is empty, let alone if there are tenants living in it. That said, I have purchased properties in very undesirable areas because they can often make the most rental profit.

In these instances I am able to recognise whether a property, although in an undesirable area, will still be sought after by tenants. If this is the case, they generally are not vandalism hotspots.

I always make a list of **all** the works that need carrying out. I make sure I take my time and list everything in every room: central heating, radiators, UPVC windows, doors, skirting boards, floor boards, wall paper stripping, painting etc.

The more properties you view and the more projects you do, the easier it gets to obtain accurate estimated costs. That said, some people might say if there is too much to do it is not worth it. I disagree because that is normally when the least amount of interest is shown by other buyers, and when you have the most scope to get a desirable price. The key is getting the property at the right price.

To run an example by you:

I viewed a property that was for sale for £90,000 and that had been fumigated the day before I viewed. It needed everything doing to it, except for the kitchen which just needed a good clean.

I offered £85,000 – it was accepted. I paid £6,700 for my builder to refurbish the property, which took 2½ weeks. I had a tenant in the day after the work was completed and remortgaged the property at 80% LTV with a surveyor's valuation of £125,000. Hence, after all my costs I got my deposit and builders costs back and managed to get an extra £9,300 in my pocket for the next project.

I have repeated this process over 20 times and have **never** not got my initial investment back plus some extra. I would say however, that in order to do this the following are crucial:

- Do your research – check comparable sales in the area which a surveyor will use to value the property. If you can't find figures, neither can your surveyor and this will make it difficult to prove what you think it should be worth.

- Open your eyes – it is easy to walk through a property and overlook many major things that need to be done. Always feel walls on the ground floor for damp, as well as ceiling walls near the roof. Look for discolouration in paint or wallpaper and always feel wallpaper to see if there are any cracks that are being hidden.

  Note the standard of the bathroom and kitchen – will cleaning them be sufficient or do they need replacing (if so, this can add significant costs).

  Always check the boiler! If it looks old and rusted – it is old and rusted and will likely need replacing which is also expensive. Finally, always get an opinion from a trusted builder. When I first started I learnt so much just by walking through a property with my builder and taking his notes.

- Learn to discern the difference between cosmetic works and construction works! The more cosmetic the work, the cheaper the project. The more construction work, the more expensive!

- Look for ways of adding additional value – is there an opportunity to create off-road parking, or put in a ground floor toilet, or tidy up the garden? What about creating open plan living areas or creating additional rooms?

- Finally, make sure you have an exit strategy – you should know exactly what you want to do with your property even before you purchase it. If you intend renting it out, then refurbish it to a suitable rental standard. If you intend selling it, then refurbish it to a suitable selling standard. There is nothing wrong with getting either letting agents or estate agents in to advise you on the refurbishment required for the relevant purpose!

By following these tips it is possible to still find properties requiring complete refurbishment which, after carrying out these works, can be remortgaged and your initial investment recovered.

I used to work on a 70% rule with these types of projects. That is to say, I would expect to get the property for 70% of its market related price in fully refurbished condition. Hence if I believe a property will be worth £125,000 after I have completed the refurbishment works, then I would not be willing to pay more than £87,500, which is 70% of £125,000.

What I would say now though, is that with lower LTV's being offered by lenders, it is necessary to get even lower prices, otherwise after remortgaging you won't get your investment funds back.

## Developing Property

One other method of making money in the current climate is through developing property. As previously mentioned in the introduction, this is not building from scratch but rather focusing on unique schemes where the shell of a building is kept, but internal re-design and layout help create multiple units within the space.

The reason I focus on these types of development schemes is because there is typically not that much cost involved in converting a shell into multiple units. It actually requires significantly more resources to build from scratch.

Total build costs can range anywhere from £80-£120 per square foot. Considering the average two-bed flat is 800 square feet, the total cost of building from scratch is between £64,000 and £96,000!

You then have to add on the cost of financing the project and the cost of land, and this can mean that to build a block of six flats you are looking at total costs well in excess of £100,000 per flat.

If you then consider trying to sell these flats, and the existing oversupply of flats as a result of developer oversupply, it is unlikely that you will achieve any profit at all by building from scratch.

I am sure any professional developers reading this will regard this quick overview is far too simplistic, and I admit costs vary substantially based on differing land costs, geographical area, and access to tradesmen and materials.

However, the point I am making is that traditional developing on brown field or green field land (where you can get planning permission) is best left to the professional.

What I am proposing is focusing on projects that not only offer scope for quick turn-around, but minimal outlay!

Let me run you through a development of this nature that I recently completed.

The property was a detached ex-housing office that was being sold at auction with a guide price of £90,000. In the weeks running up to the auction I had kept my eye on the lot and found out from the auctioneer that the council, which was selling the property, was going to drop the price due to lack of interest.

As it turned out, the property ended up not selling on the day and I subsequently made a viewing and quickly saw that the property offered a relatively easy conversion project. There was virtually no construction work to be carried out except for putting in some internal acoustic walls and some new windows. Otherwise, it seemed a straightforward enough project.

I estimated the total works to carry out the conversion would cost £60,000 and would take around three months to complete. I also worked out that by converting the property into three two-bedroom self-contained flats, I could expect to achieve re-sale values of between £85,000 and £95,000 per property.

So by spending a total of £150,000 (including £80,000 to buy the property and £10,000 in finance costs) I could end up making a profit of £120,000! Even better, with the current housing price crash, if I was not able to sell the properties at my estimated asking prices, I could remortgage each flat individually, rent them out and still end up with £63,750 in my pocket, while also making decent rental income.

There were some complications, for example I would need to obtain planning permission to convert the property from offices to flats. There was also a clause in the auction contract requiring the purchaser to pay the council 5% of the agreed purchase price towards their legal fees – this is quite common when council properties are sold so keep your eye's peeled.

I did, however, manage to use these complications to my advantage. I made an offer subject to completion only once I had obtained the relevant planning permission. The planning permission took 3½ months to come through which, if I had bought at auction, I would have had to finance with bridging finance at around 1.5% per month.

As such I saved myself just under £4,000 in interest charges.

Another point to note is that, while obtaining quotes from builders, even through I gave them drawings and specification sheets drawn up by my architect, I ended up getting estimates as high as £140,000! I must say, I thought I was in trouble when I got this estimate but my faith in British builders was restored when I eventually received two quotes in the region of £50,000 each.

So at least I knew my costings were accurate. If I had accepted the first quote I would have lost a lot of money!

The actual build went without any major problems and I ended up having the properties sold within 2½ months of completing the purchase. I did offer the builder an incentive to finish early and this helped me save money by not having to pay an additional month's bridging finance.

I ended up making a tidy sum close to my original estimate and moved quickly on to my next project!

Now you may think that this is the end of the story but it is not!

Using my traditional buy-to-let finance brain I had always limited my developments to a size at which I felt comfortable committing to a deposit amount.

However, what I only realized later in my property career is that, in as many ways that you can finance a property purchase, you can also find ways of financing bigger projects with limited resources.

To explain, if I look at a development which involves buying a property for £500,000, with additional build and financing costs of £300,000, I would have thought this was impossible early on in my property career. What I eventually learnt was that it is possible to get involved with these types of deals, without even having to commit a single penny of your own resources!

So I found it was possible to look at development projects which, once completed, offered the potential to make hundreds of thousands of pounds! So many landlords do not realize this and exclude these types of projects from their future plans. Let me illustrate it slightly differently.

What would you prefer:

- To carry out a string of 10 property refurbishment projects and/or below market value purchases over a year, managing these over the year and hoping to extract £5,000 per property after investment costs have been recouped after remortgaging?

OR

- To focus on one development project which will take you four months to complete and will make you at least £80,000 in profit?

I know where I will be focusing my efforts in the near term and it won't be buying new properties with the hope of getting relatively small cash amounts back after remortgaging, with house prices dropping by perhaps 20% over the next two years!

My strategy going forward is to focus on high profit development deals and part of that is due to my goal of securing the best remortgage deals available through being able to prove a high income and, where necessary, using my cash reserves from development projects to improve my rental profits, and also hold cash reserves for any future mortgage interest rate shocks.

I also intend to be in a strong position when the market eventually begins to recover, which will likely be when mortgage finance returns after banks adjust to their current mega losses.

When house prices start to recover, that is when I will begin purchasing again and stand to make significant gains through capital appreciation. Until that point I will be focusing on generating cash through profitable developments.

Now many of you may be wondering exactly how I am able to source these types of developments and even how I can finance them with not having to invest any of my own money.

I will tell you that there are more and more of these types of profitable developments becoming available, some more complex than others due to planning and building regulation conditions.

Not only are these developments coming up through traditional means such as commercial and residential estate agents and auctions, but more developers are relinquishing their land banks and development stocks to free up capital to complete existing projects.

So to find these deals you need to be looking at commercial and residential estate agents and more importantly at auctions.

It is not through using other investors funds or pooling a group of investors spare cash that I can do these developments. It is through specialist lenders that provide development funding. Typically these lenders offer a percentage of the Gross Development Value (GDV) to finance the purchase, development and build costs.

The GDV is the total re-sale value of all the units or properties once the development has been completed and you can typically obtain finance at 75% LTV right up to 100% of the build and purchase costs.

The higher the LTV, the more expensive the funding. So for instance, if you took out a 75% development loan, you would typically be charged between 1.25% to 1.5% of the total loan outstanding per month. If you took a higher percentage out you would pay up to 1.95% interest per month on the outstanding loan amount which can be very expensive.

You can find these lenders through searching on Google with the keywords "residential development funding".

If there is one thing I hope you have learnt from this book thus far it is that being a landlord is a dynamic experience. You will have to think on your feet and explore different ways of reacting positively to the challenges brought on by the credit crunch.

Lying down and giving up is not an option for me, and neither should it be for you. I would challenge you to think in different and dynamic ways, especially when you feel you have run out of options, and I have found it is when I am most desperate that I find the best solution.

# CHAPTER 13

# **Conclusion**

The current economic climate is presenting challenges to landlords on a number of fronts and it is imperative that action is taken to ensure survival.

The starting point is to ascertain the current health of your property portfolio, as well as clearly identifying a strategy going forward, bearing in mind certain key considerations.

Landlords need to understand the current mortgage market, as well as the impact of the credit crunch and likely future consequences.

The impact of potential interest rate changes on your property portfolio over the next 12–18 months is crucial to understand.

This includes knowing exactly what mortgage products are available to you, when your current mortgage deals expire, what SVR will apply, when to begin looking for new remortgages, and ensuring your credit report is clean.

Landlords will also need to make sure they are getting the right level of rents, increasing rents where possible, maximising yields, keeping voids to an absolute minimum, and targeting new groups of tenants.

Landlords will also have to find ways of increasing deposits and protecting them, as well as considering joining various tenancy deposit schemes, and perhaps even considering unique ways of protecting their deposits.

The ability to decrease or minimise increases in operating costs will also be key, with the potential savings from self-management of a portfolio being a key area of improvement. Where self-management is utilised it will be important to keep running costs to a minimum and ensure effective time management.

Landlords will have to make difficult decisions relating to whether they should sell any of their properties, with consideration to the often overlooked costs involved with this and balancing the need for raising cash against their existing financial resources and medium to long term investment goals.

Landlords will also have to concentrate on other areas including reining in personal expenditure, improving personal mortgages, reducing personal debt, considering interest rate insurance, getting their taxes in order and constantly reviewing their existing portfolio to maximise portfolio returns and ensure they are aware of any short to medium-term cash flow shocks.

Finally, landlords will need to be creative in finding and exploiting new ways of making money in property whether this be through buying high yielding investment properties, below market value methods, buying properties requiring major refurbishment and/or developing property.

I trust that you have learnt from this guide how to improve your returns from your current portfolio, whether it be just one buy-to-let property or 150, and I wish you success in the coming years.

**Toby Hone**

# Pay Less Tax!

...with help from Taxcafe's unique tax guides and software

<u>All products available online at</u>
**<u>www.taxcafe.co.uk/books</u>**

**How to Avoid Property Tax**
**By Carl Bayley BSc ACA**

*How to Avoid Property Tax* is widely regarded as *the* tax bible for property investors. This unique and bestselling guide is jam packed with ideas that will save you thousands in income tax and capital gains tax.

*"A valuable guide to the tax issues facing buy-to-let investors"* - **THE INDEPENDENT**

**How to Avoid Tax on Foreign Property**
**By Carl Bayley BSc ACA**

Find out everything you need to know about paying less tax on overseas property. Completely up to date with key UK and overseas tax changes.

## Using a Property Company to Save Tax
## By Carl Bayley

Currently a 'hot topic' for the serious property investor, this guide shows how you can significantly boost your after-tax returns by setting up your own property company and explains ALL the tax consequences of property company ownership.

*"An excellent tax resource....informative and clearly written"* **The Letting Update Journal**

---

## Keeping It Simple
## By James Smith BSc ACA

This plain-English guide tells you everything you need to know about small business bookkeeping, accounting, tax returns and VAT.

---

## Property Capital Gains Tax Calculator
## By Carl Bayley

This powerful piece of software will calculate in seconds the capital gains tax payable when you sell a property and help you cut the tax bill. It provides tax planning tips based on your personal circumstances and a concise summary and detailed breakdown of all calculations.

---

## Non-Resident & Offshore Tax Planning
## By Lee Hadnum LLB ACA CTA

By becoming non-resident or moving your assets offshore it is possible to cut your tax bill to zero. This guide explains what you have to do and all the traps to avoid. Also contains detailed info on using offshore trusts and companies.

*"The ultimate guide to legal tax avoidance"* **Shelter Offshore**

---

## The World's Best Tax Havens
## By Lee Hadnum

This book provides a fascinating insight into the glamorous world of tax havens and how you can use them to cut your taxes to zero and safeguard your financial freedom.

---

## How to Avoid Inheritance Tax
## By Carl Bayley

Making sure you adequately plan for inheritance tax could save you literally hundreds of thousands of pounds. *How to Avoid Inheritance Tax* is a unique guide which will tell you all you need to know about sheltering your family's money from the taxman. This guide is essential reading for parents, grandparents and adult children.

*"Useful source of Inheritance Tax information"* **What Investment Magazine**

---

### Using a Company to Save Tax
### By Lee Hadnum

By running your business through a limited company you stand to save tens of thousands of pounds in tax and national insurance every year. This tax guide tells you everything you need to know about the tax benefits of incorporation.

### Salary versus Dividends
### By Carl Bayley

This unique guide is essential reading for anyone running their business as a limited company. After reading it, you will know the most tax efficient way in which to extract funds from your company, and save thousands in tax!

### Selling Your Business
### By Lee Hadnum

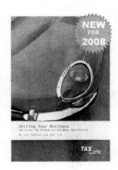

This guide tells you everything you need to know about paying less tax and maximizing your profits when you sell your business. It is essential reading for anyone selling a company or sole trader business.

## How to Avoid Tax on Your Stock Market Profits
## By Lee Hadnum

This tax guide can only be described as THE definitive tax-saving resource for stock market investors and traders. Anyone who owns shares, unit trusts, ISAs, corporate bonds or other financial assets should read it as it contains a huge amount of unique tax planning information.

## How to Profit from Off-Plan Property
## By Alyssa and David Savage

This property investment guide tells you everything you need to know about investing in off-plan and new-build property. It contains a fascinating insight into how you can make big money from off-plan property... and avoid all the pitfalls along the way.

## How to Build a £4 Million Property Portfolio:
### Lifetime Lessons of a Student Landlord
## By Tony Bayliss

Tony Bayliss is one of the UK's most successful student property investors. In *How to Build a £4 Million Property Portfolio* he reveals all his secrets – how he picks the best and most profitable student properties; how he markets his properties and how he enjoys capital growth of 12% pa, year in year out.

# Disclaimer

1. Please note that this guide is intended as general guidance only for individual readers and does NOT constitute accountancy, tax, investment or other professional advice. Neither Taxcafe UK Limited nor the author can accept any responsibility or liability for loss which may arise from reliance on information contained in this guide.

2. Please note that legislation, the law and practices by government and regulatory authorities are constantly changing. We therefore recommend that for legal, accountancy, tax, investment or other professional advice, you consult a suitably qualified accountant, tax specialist, independent financial adviser, or other professional adviser. Please also note that your personal circumstances may vary from the general examples given in this guide  and your professional adviser will be able to give specific advice based on your personal circumstances.

3. Please note that Taxcafe UK Limited has relied wholly on the expertise of the author in the preparation of the content of this Tax Guide. The author is not an employee of Taxcafe UK Limited but has been selected by Taxcafe UK Limited using reasonable care and skill to write the content of this Tax Guide.